T0291280

The Role of Governments in Markets

This shortform book presents key peer-reviewed research selected by expert series editors and contextualised by new analysis from each author on government intervention and unexpected consequences in industrial history.

With contributions on organisational structure, the quality of corporate governance, protectionism, the shareholder value model, and economic nationalism, this volume provides an array of fascinating insights into industrial history.

Of interest to business and economic historians, this shortform book also provides analysis and illustrative case studies that will be valuable reading across the social sciences.

John F. Wilson is Pro Vice-Chancellor (Business and Law) at Northumbria University at Newcastle, UK. He has published widely in the fields of business, management and industrial history, including ten monographs, six edited collections and over seventy articles and chapters.

Steven Toms spent fifteen years in senior management at Nottingham University, UK, as head of the undergraduate programme, chair of teaching committee and research director before becoming Head of York Management School in 2004.

Ian Jones is a Senior Research Assistant at Newcastle Business School, Northumbria University, UK.

Routledge Focus on Industrial History
Series Editors: John F. Wilson, Steven Toms
and Ian Jones

This Shortform series presents key peer-reviewed research originally published in the *Journal of Industrial History*, selected by expert series editors and contextualised by new analysis from each author on how the specific field addressed has evolved.

Of interest to business historians, economic historians and social scientists interested in the development of key industries, the series makes theoretical and conceptual contributions to the field, as well as providing a plethora of empirical, illustrative and detailed case-studies of industrial developments in Britain, the United States and other international settings.

Management and Industry
Case Studies in UK Industrial History
Edited by John F. Wilson, Nicholas D. Wong and Steven Toms

The Cotton and Textiles Industry: Innovation and Maturity
Case Studies in Industrial History
Edited by John F. Wilson, Steven Toms and Nicholas D. Wong

The Cotton and Textiles Industry: Managing Decline
Case Studies in Industrial History
Edited by John F. Wilson, Steven Toms and Nicholas D. Wong

The Role of Governments in Markets
Interventions and Unexpected Consequences in Industrial History
Edited by John F. Wilson, Steven Toms and Ian Jones

A Search for Competitive Advantage
Case Studies in Industrial History
Edited by John F. Wilson, Steven Toms and Ian Jones

For more information about this series, please visit: www.routledge.com/
Routledge-Focus-on-Industrial-History/book-series/RFIH

The Role of Governments in Markets

Interventions and Unexpected
Consequences in Industrial History

**Edited by John F. Wilson, Steven Toms
and Ian Jones**

LONDON AND NEW YORK

First published 2021
by Routledge
2 Park Square, Milton Park, Abingdon, Oxon OX14 4RN

and by Routledge
605 Third Avenue, New York, NY 10158

Routledge is an imprint of the Taylor & Francis Group, an informa business

© 2021 selection and editorial matter, John F. Wilson, Steven Toms and Ian Jones; individual chapters, the contributors

The right of John F. Wilson, Steven Toms and Ian Jones to be identified as the authors of the editorial material, and of the authors for their individual chapters, has been asserted in accordance with sections 77 and 78 of the Copyright, Designs and Patents Act 1988.

British Library Cataloguing-in-Publication Data
A catalogue record for this book is available from the British Library

Library of Congress Cataloging-in-Publication Data
Names: Wilson, J. F., editor. | Jones, Ian (Senior research assistant), editor. | Toms, Steven, editor.
Title: The role of governments in markets : interventions and unexpected consequences in industrial history / John Wilson, Steven Tom and Ian Jones.
Description: Abingdon, Oxon ; New York, NY : Routledge, 2021. | Series: Routledge focus on industrial history | Includes bibliographical references and index.
Subjects: LCSH: Industrial policy—History. | Industries—History.
Classification: LCC HD3611 .R7234 2021 (print) | LCC HD3611 (ebook) | DDC 338.9009—dc23
LC record available at https://lccn.loc.gov/2021006971
LC ebook record available at https://lccn.loc.gov/2021006972

ISBN: 978-0-367-02406-2 (hbk)
ISBN: 978-1-032-05298-4 (pbk)
ISBN: 978-0-429-39980-0 (ebk)

Typeset in Times New Roman
by Apex CoVantage, LLC

Contents

Figures

Tables

Contributors

Peter Scott is Professor of International Business History at Henley Business School, University of Reading. He has published extensively on household consumption, consumer durables, and the housebuilding sector. He has published four books, with the most recent being *The Market Makers: Creating Mass Markets for Consumer Durables in Inter-War Britain* (2017).

Tim Rooth was Emeritus Professor of Modern Economic History at Portsmouth University until his retirement in 2005. He published works on international trade and had a particular interest in Canada, serving as president of the British Association of Canadian Studies from 2002 to 2004, editing a volume for its 4th anniversary titled *Canadian Studies in Britain 1970–2000: An Assessment in the Context of a Changing World.*

Patrick Crowhurst completed his PhD at Queen Mary College, University of London, and was a Visiting Fellow at the University of Leicester. He has published two books on the history of Czechoslovakia: *A History of Czechoslovakia Between the Wars: From Versailles to Hitler's Invasion* and *Hitler and Czechoslovakia in World War II.*

Meng Li completed his PhD at the Japanese Advanced Institute of Science and Technology in 2003.

Sue Bowden is Professor of Modern Economic History at the Department of Economics at the University of York and was President of the Association of Business Historians from 2004–2005. She has published works on corporate governance, consumer durables, and developing economies in Africa.

Andrew Gamble is the Professor of Politics in the Department of Politics and International Relations at the University of Sheffield, having formerly also worked as the Professor of Politics at Queens College,

University of Cambridge. He has published extensively on a wide range of political topics including political theory and ideology, corporate governance, ownership, and stakeholding. He has published 22 books including, most recently, *Politics: Why It Matters* and *Can the Welfare State Survive?*

Introduction

Purpose and significance of the series

The concept of the Routledge Focus on Industrial History series was motivated by the desire of the editors to provide an outlet for articles originally published in the defunct *Journal of Industrial History* (*JIH*). By using an extensive repository of top-quality publications, the series will ensure that the authors' findings contribute to recent debates in the field of management and industrial history. Indeed, the articles contained in these volumes will appeal to a wide audience, including business historians, economic historians and social scientists interested in longitudinal studies of the development of key industries and themes. Moreover, the series will provide fresh insight into how the academic field has developed over the past 20 years.

The editors believe that the quality of scholarship evident in the articles originally published in the *JIH* now deserve a much broader audience. The peer-reviewed articles are built on robust business-historical research methodologies and are subject to extensive primary research. The series will make important theoretical and conceptual contributions to the field and provide a plethora of empirical, illustrative and detailed case studies of industrial developments in the United Kingdom, the United States and other international settings. The collection will be of interest to a broad stratum of social scientists, especially business school and history department academics, because it provides valuable material that can be used in both teaching and research.

Building on the original *Journal of Industrial History*

The first edition of the *Journal of Industrial History* was published in 1998, with the aim of providing 'clear definitional parameters for industrial historians' and in turn establishing links between 'industrial history and theoretical work in social science disciplines like economics, management (including international business), political science, sociology, and anthropology'. Because it has been more than 20 years since its original publication, it is clear that the relevance of the *JIH* has stood the test of time. The original *JIH* volumes covered a diverse range of topics, including industrial structure and behaviour, especially in manufacturing and services; industrial and business case studies; business strategy and structure; nationalisation and privatisation; globalisation and competitive advantage; business culture and industrial development; education, training and human resources; industrial relations and its institutions; the relationship between financial institutions and industry; industrial politics, including the formulation and impact of industrial and commercial policy; and industry and technology. The current Routledge Focus on Industrial History series will provide a cross-section of articles that cover a wide range of themes and topics, many of which remain central to management studies. These include separate volumes: *Management and Industry*; *Banking and Finance*; and *Growth and Decline of American Industry*. Future volumes in the series will cover case studies in sources of competitive advantage, knowledge management; the development of professional management, and the cotton and textile industry. The Routledge Focus on Industrial History series will reframe highly original material that illustrates a wide variety of themes in management and organisation studies, including entrepreneurship, strategy, family business, trust, networks and international business, focusing on topics such as the growth of the firm, crisis management, governance, management and leadership.

Volume five: contribution and key findings

The fifth volume of this series focuses on the role of the government in markets and the unexpected consequences of intervention. This volume examines a broad range of government interventions into markets through the twentieth century spanning Britain, Czechoslovakia and Japan. The articles in this volume show the intent behind these interventions, the short- and long-term effects they had, and how individuals and organisations attempted to circumvent the intentions of government policies.

The first chapter, 'Protectionism and the growth of overseas multinational enterprise in interwar Britain' is a study by Peter Scott sand Tim Rooth that analyses the effects of British tariffs in the inter-war years on foreign direct investment (FDI) in Britain and inward investment from British businesses. This chapter highlights how tariffs and imperial preference policies pre-1938 positively impacted FDI, encouraging foreign firms to invest in British-based production to avoid tariffs and to access Britain's large domestic and Empire markets. The devaluation of the pound sterling after abandoning the gold standard, the lack of bureaucracy when establishing a business in

Britain, and the generally poor perception of British firms abroad also convinced many foreign firms that they would be able to outcompete domestic producers. The chapter also shows how British firms could take advantage of tariffs by using the expectation of greater profits to invest in their production, as well as to merge with foreign firms to benefit from their knowledge and capital.

The second chapter, 'The making of the First Czechoslovak Republic and the national control of companies: the nostrification policy and economic nationalism, 1918–1938' by Patrick Crowhurst, focuses on the attempts by the newly formed Czechoslovak Republic to ensure that the owners of its industries supported the nation-building project. As part of the nostrification policy, businesses operating inside Czechoslovakia had to maintain their headquarters inside the country and control of the capital of these firms had to be by a majority of Czech citizens. Crowhurst shows the methods that the owners of the firms used to circumvent the nostrification policies, as well as the harm that these laws could inflict on Czech markets as well as the firms themselves. Although these laws intended to ensure that firms operating inside Czechoslovakia supported the nation-building effort, the results were the continuation of foreign control of firms, the exploitation of the Czech market by these foreign-owned firms for greater profits due to a lack of competition, and difficulties for Czech-owned firms in accessing foreign capital and knowledge to make themselves competitive.

The third chapter, 'The making of a puzzling industry: historical perspectives on Japan's petrochemical industry' by Meng Li, analyses the rapid development and sudden stagnation of the Japanese petrochemical industry post World War II. Li shows how government intervention that directed the growth and expansion of the firms producing petrochemicals had short-term benefits. By limiting expansion and only periodically allowing newcomers to begin production, the Japanese government ensured that newcomers could enjoy the benefits of the knowledge accrued by earlier entrants, whilst the earlier entrants were given preference when permission to expand their operations was given and could benefit financially from the lack of competition in the market. However, this slow and controlled expansion had negative long-term effects. Japanese firms were unable to expand quickly enough to compete internationally, whilst smaller domestic producers survived as they were protected from domestic competition by government policy that restricted expansion through acquisition and mergers.

The final chapter, 'Corporate governance and public policy: "new" initiatives by "Old" Labour to reform stakeholder behaviour in the UK, 1956–1969' by Sue Bowden and Andrew Gamble, discusses attempts by the British government, under Harold Wilson, to reform corporate governance and restructure British industry. This chapter focuses on two aims of the government: to increase the size of British firms through mergers that would allow them to compete internationally, and to improve the quality of management to make the best use of new technologies and the greater size of these firms. Bowden and Gamble first show the government's attempts to reform corporate governance by re-thinking what the rights and responsibilities of shareholders should be, with discussions taking place on the idea of the 'stakeholder firm'. These discussions, eventually shelved, aimed to encourage shareholders to be more active in influencing the management of firms rather than treating their shares as an asset to be held to receive dividends and traded when profitable. The chapter then discusses the government's role in encouraging, supporting, and directly influencing mergers between firms. The chapter concludes by showing how the government's actions in encouraging and supporting mergers undermined the idea of stakeholder firms and encouraged the types of behaviour they had originally planned to discourage, that of treating shares only as assets to be traded with no responsibility to the firm.

Conclusion

It is apparent from this brief review of the chapters that the fifth volume in the series makes important contributions to the field of industrial history in several ways. Firstly, it provides a series of high calibre and unique studies in aspects of industrial history that contribute to more recent debates on the government's role in markets, corporate governance, protectionism, the shareholder value model, and the rights and responsibilities of ownership. Secondly, the chapters shed light on the broader subjects of innovation, organisational structure, organisational networks, co-operation and competition, and nationalism as a force that shapes both markets and organisations. Finally, this volume provides strong historical case-studies that can be used by students and researchers who are exploring issues related to the evolving role of government in markets in Britain, Europe and Japan, as well as the intended and unintended effects of this intervention. The editors believe that this volume will not only provide a much wider audience for articles that link into a range of topical issues but also feed into debates in the wider social sciences. These are themes that will be developed further in subsequent volumes of the Routledge Series of Industrial History, highlighting the intrinsic value in republishing material from the *Journal of Industrial History* and ensuring that the articles contribute extensively to current debates.

1 Protectionism and the growth of overseas multinational enterprise in interwar Britain*

Peter Scott and Tim Rooth

One of the key features of Britain's twentieth century industrial development has been the expansion of overseas multinational enterprises. These have come to dominate a number of major capital-intensive industries, while making an important contribution to a wide range of British industrial production. The interwar period saw a considerable increase in the scale and scope of overseas multinationals in Britain, with several hundred new plants being established. This article examines the influence of Britain's increasingly protectionist trading regime in stimulating this foreign direct investment (fdi) into Britain, and assesses the economic impact of tariff-induced inward investment.

The introduction of very selective tariff protection from 1915 is shown to have acted as an important stimulus to fdi in the sectors covered, encouraging the establishment of branch plants which were of considerable importance to the development of a range of 'high-tech', capital-intensive industries. The move to comprehensive tariffs from November 1931 led to a mushrooming of fdi, diversifying production in a broader range of industries and introducing new technologies, production methods and design standards. The stimulus to fdi induced by protectionism is shown to have exerted a positive influence on the British economy, especially in the long-term. This reinforces the findings of more general recent studies that, contrary to earlier analyses, the impact of the General Tariff on the British economy was positive and significant.

Early trade barriers and inward fdi

Since the late nineteenth century Britain has been the recipient of substantial direct investment by foreign manufacturers. During the decades prior to 1914 it maintained one of the most radically free-trade policies of any major industrial nation. However, there is evidence that as early as the 1890s fears of future tariffs may have influenced some companies, such as Western

Electric, to establish UK plants.[1] Britain's own (extremely few) tariffs also stimulated some fdi, for example selected import duties on 'luxury' food items such as chocolates induced the German chocolate manufacturer Gebr. Stollwerck to establish UK production.[2] There is also evidence that the emergence of imperial preference encouraged German firms to invest in the UK, to take advantage of easier selling conditions in the British Dominions. While Britain retained its free trade stance, from 1897 Canada granted unilateral preferential treatment to goods produced in Britain and over the next decade similar concessions were introduced by South Africa, New Zealand, and Australia.[3]

Although there were virtually no UK tariffs prior to the First World War, non-tariff barriers did play a part in encouraging inward investment. The Patent and Design Act of 1907, which provided for the revocation of patents not worked in the UK within four years of their registration, caused a number of American, German, and Swiss firms to manufacture in Britain, in industries such as chemicals, cinematic film, electrical products, safety razor blades, cash registers, and optical glass.[4] 'Buy British' campaigns were a frequent motive for defensive German investments in the UK, while other relevant non-tariff barriers included British government discrimination in favour of UK-produced goods, and early forms of local content rules.[5] Most other industrialised nations embraced protectionism much more rapidly and completely than Britain. Protectionism's role in stimulating fdi during this period is widely recognised in both empirical and theoretical work on the growth of multinational enterprise; for example Jones has argued that the spread of tariffs and other trade barriers before 1914 constituted the most important international stimulus to the replacement of exporting by direct investment.[6]

From the First World War Britain began to introduce protectionist measures. The first major move was the McKenna duties, imposed in 1915 to raise revenue and save shipping space: 33.3 per cent ad valorem tariffs were levied on gramophones, clocks, watches, cinematograph film and certain motor vehicles and components. Although ostensibly emergency war-time measures, they were subsequently renewed until absorbed into the general tariff in 1938. More avowedly protectionist were two pieces of legislation enacted in 1921, the Dyestuffs Act, which prohibited dyestuffs imports except under licence, and, of wider application, the Safeguarding of Industries Act. The coverage of 'safeguarding' was extended at various times during the 1920s, and in 1925 silk duties, which included artificial silk, added to the tariff walls. By the end of the decade protection was still modest, almost 85 per cent of imports entering duty free.[7] Nonetheless, its sectoral incidence proved a powerful inducement for fdi.

The 1920s saw a substantial increase in inward fdi; it has been estimated that 167 new manufacturing subsidiaries of overseas firms were established in Britain during the decade, compared to 76 from 1900 to 1909 and 58 from 1910 to 1919.[8] The new tariffs were influential in leading a number of major foreign-based companies (particularly American firms, which made up over three quarters of new multinationals in Britain during the 1920s) either to establish British plants or expand their existing UK activities.[9] In 1929 the Manager of the Slough Estate, a major centre for multinationals, stated 'At least twenty of our 116 firms have come here as a result . . . It has sometimes been suggested that a statue of Mr McKenna should be erected in a prominent place here'.[10]

The 1925 silk duties attracted a number of foreign companies, including Dutch-based Enka (1925) and German-owned British Bemberg (1926).[11] Further investments followed: the German manufacturer R. Schaerf decided that higher UK labour costs 'would be more than counterbalanced by the duty . . . on artificial silk fabrics and that it would be cheaper to produce the goods here than abroad.'[12] Similar calculations were made by Dutch businessman C. F. M. Verstynen, who estimated that under the new duties, '1s per lb is saved by having a factory here, although 4d or 5d of that 1s goes in higher wages'.[13]

The McKenna duties were an important factor behind inward direct investment in the British motor vehicle industry. The duties had been scrapped in 1924 by the Labour government but were re-instated the following year by Baldwin's new administration. This appears to have persuaded a number of companies that the duties were here to stay. Ford had already decided that the tariffs were likely to be maintained and had moved to 100 per cent UK production prior to their suspension; but their re-imposition proved a powerful stimulant for other companies.[14] Alfred Sloan of General Motors, convinced that the McKenna duties raised a formidable barrier to all foreign vehicles, authorised negotiations with Austin before settling on the acquisition of Vauxhall in 1925.[15] Citroën, stating that the duties made it impossible to compete on price with several British makes, commenced manufacture in Slough.[16] The Board of Trade also noted that moves to UK assembly or manufacture by the Hudson Essex Co., Willis Overland Co., Renault, Fiat, and Hispano-Suiza, had followed the introduction or re-imposition of the duties.[17]

The addition of rubber tyres to the McKenna list in 1927 induced major manufacturers, such as Firestone (which was paying £15,000 per week in import duties), Goodyear, the India Tyre & Rubber Co., the Overman Cushion Tyre Co., Michelin, and Pirelli, to leap the tariff walls by establishing UK factories or acquiring existing UK manufacturers.[18] A number of other overseas tyre manufacturers, such as the Seiberling Rubber Co., responded to the tariffs by making arrangements with British companies to produce their tyres.[19]

In addition to the growth of tariffs, Britain's continued openness to overseas enterprises provided a further attraction for foreign multinationals. It was seen as a country with relatively red-tape-free attitudes to overseas firms, cultural proximity to America (which dominated inward fdi during this decade), a large internal market, and export links to the Empire and continental Europe.[20] For example, in 1929 the Electric Hose and Rubber Co. stated that its decision to establish a factory at Watford would produce considerable savings as, 'The Colonies are big buyers . . . there is a heavier duty on American goods taken into British Colonies than there is on goods sent from this country'.[21] Meanwhile an intensification of nationalistic sentiment, expressed in an invigorated 'Buy British' movement – which encompassed local and central government, many corporations, and individual consumers – placed further pressure on overseas manufacturers to service the UK market via British production.[22]

The Emergency Tariff and inward fdi

Following the 1931 economic crisis the new National Government undertook two actions which, together, had a profound effect on the flow of foreign-based enterprises to Britain: taking sterling off the gold standard (the impact of which is discussed below), and moving towards comprehensive protectionism. The Abnormal Importations Act, introduced in November 1931 (presented as emergency legislation, necessitated by 'dumping') imposed ad valorem duties of 50 per cent or more.[23] Coming in the wake of sterling's depreciation, this proved a powerful stimulus to fdi, particularly since the high duties appeared to foreshadow a severely protectionist regime. The legislation was seen as a holding operation until a more considered tariff schedule could be introduced, but the constraints placed on the protectionist Conservatives having to operate within a National Government containing free-traders necessitated a degree of compromise.[24] Hence when the Import Duties Act came into force in March 1932 the initial level of duties was low, the standard rate on most finished manufactures being set at a modest 10 per cent. Consequently some new foreign-based companies complained of inadequate protection and several withdrew from negotiations for starting production.[25] However, the Import Duties Advisory Committee, the independent body established under the Import Duties Act, quickly acted to raise tariff levels; its first order increased tariffs on most finished manufactures to 20 per cent and imposed higher rates on selected 'luxuries' and some other products.[26] Other recommendations followed rapidly, increasingly tending to supplement or replace ad valorem tariffs by specific duties to target cheap imports.[27] These could produce spectacular levels of protection.

One consequence was a sharp fall in manufactured imports. Another was a dramatic rise in inward investment. Within a few weeks of the Emergency Tariff's announcement a large number of firms had expressed interest in establishing UK production.[28] The Board of Trade's Chief Industrial Advisor's office (CIA) undertook the responsibility of collating applications, and advising whether each application was in Britain's interest. From November 1931 to the middle of April 1932, 391 cases of firms entering into negotiations to establish British factories were recorded (not all of which led to plants being opened). It was noted that, as a foreign company was free to set up production without consulting any government department if it did not wish to import foreign personnel, this figure was probably an underestimate. 205 of the 391 firms were German. Other important countries were Belgium (37), the USA (27), and Switzerland (21). 227 firms fell into six industrial groups: textiles (76), hosiery (50), other clothing (25), leather (30), the radio industry (23) and other electrical goods (23).[29] 70 cases were also recorded of British manufacturers considering establishing new undertakings, or extending existing plants, with the assistance of foreign key workers.

Data on those firms which actually commenced production during the 18 months following the Abnormal Importations Act were published, as parliamentary answers, at six-monthly intervals. The figures, shown in Table 1.1, indicate that fdi was concentrated in the immediate aftermath of the Emergency Tariff announcement. During the six months following the tariff the number of firms entering Britain averaged about 20.5 per month; the monthly average fell to 15.5 during the next six months, and 9.5 in the six months from October 1932. Longer-term data, restricted to firms with an initial employment of 25 or more, confirms the considerable short-term boost which the tariff provided to fdi, foreign-based plants accounting for almost 20 per cent

Table 1.1 New foreign firms in Britain, November 1931 – April 1933 and their employment

Period	No. of firms	Employment (UK)	Employment (foreign key workers)
November 1931 to April 1932	123*	3,882	370
May to October 1932	95**	3,465	245
Total end October 1932	N/A	9,361	N/A
November 1932 to April 1933	57	1,533	N/A
Total end April 1933	254	10,883	N/A

Source: House of Commons, *Parliamentary Debates*, Vol. 266 (1932), cols. 1331–34; Vol. 273 (1932), cols 734–37; Vol. 278 (1933), cols 917–19.

Notes: * Refers to the end of the first week of May 1932.
** Refers to the period from the end of the first week of May 1932 to the end of October.

of new plants in Britain during 1932, but less than five per cent from 1935–8, as is shown in Figure 1.1.

Table 1.2 shows the national distribution of the 218 firms entering Britain during the first year of the tariff, together with that for multinationals

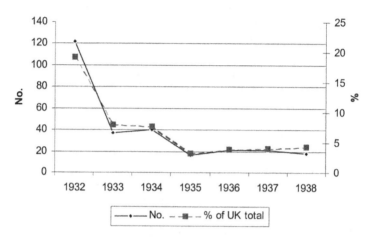

Figure 1.1 New foreign plants employing 25 or more people established in Britain during 1932–1938, number and proportion of all new plants

Source: Board of Trade, *Survey of Industrial Development* (London: HMSO, 1934–1939).

Table 1.2 The distribution of foreign plants established in Britain between November 1931 and October 1932, and during the 1920s, by country of origin

Country of origin	(1)	(2)	Total	1920–9
Germany	65	40	105	6
France	11	7	18	7
Austria	11	N/A	N/A	0
Belgium	9	6	15	0
USA	9	10	19	127
Holland	6	7	13	14
Switzerland	N/A	6	N/A	2
Italy	N/A	2	N/A	1
Hungary	N/A	2	N/A	1
Czechoslovakia	N/A	2	N/A	0
Other	12	13	25	9
Total	123	95	218	167

Source: House of Commons, *Parliamentary Debates*, Vol. 266 (1932), col. 1331; Vol. 273 (1932), col. 337; Bostock & Jones database.

Notes: (1) November 1931 to end of first week of May 1932
(2) End of first week of May 1932 to end of October 1932.
'Total' represents November 1931 to October 1932.

arriving during the 1920s.[30] The tariff had produced a substantial change in the composition of fdi source countries in favour of Western Europe. German companies made up 48.2 per cent of entrants, in contrast to the 1920s when they accounted for only 3.6 per cent. Similarly Austria and Belgium, which had not undertaken any fdi in Britain during the 1920s, became substantial source countries. The increasing importance of these three countries appears to be closely linked to the sectoral incidence of the tariff. The Austrian and Belgian firms were dominated by manufacturers in three sectors previously almost entirely untouched by UK tariffs – the clothing, textile, and leather industries; these also accounted for around 42 per cent of German firms (meanwhile around 44 per cent of German entrants operated in relatively 'high-tech' industries such as electrical goods, instrument engineering, chemicals, plastics, and safety razor-blades).[31]

The clothing, textile, and leather goods industries in these countries had experienced depression since the 1920s. The imposition of high British tariffs simultaneously provided a 'push' factor for fdi, by restricting access to a major overseas market, and a 'pull' factor, as, once operating in Britain, they would enjoy the benefits of a protected market in which domestic producers were not perceived to be particularly competitive. As the Czech hosiery manufacturer Eric Pasold recalled, devaluation and tariffs threatened to terminate his British sales, 'but where would the British get those millions of dozens of fleecy knickers from? I gathered there were very few Terrot-type knitting machines in the country . . . British manufacturers did not have a reputation for being very efficient . . . this would be the right time to establish . . . an ultra-modern knitting mill, in England.'[32]

US firms, which had comprised 76.0 per cent of fdi during the 1920s, accounted for only 8.7 per cent of new overseas firms in the year following the Emergency Tariff. This may have been influenced by the Depression, which hit American industry with particular severity, domestic financial problems forcing many US corporations to curtail overseas expansion.[33] Many had Canadian subsidiaries, through which they were able to export to Britain without incurring the new tariffs. Others set up Canadian branch plants in the early 1930s, partly in response to exchange difficulties and rising Canadian tariffs, but also because of imperial preferences. In the first four months of 1932 alone, of 94 new US foreign factories, 87 were established in Canada.[34] Furthermore, in those concentrated capital-intensive sectors where US corporations had the strongest relative advantage, firms were often able to respond to the new conditions with cartel arrangements: during the 1930s in a range of industries firm strategy shifted from fdi to international collusive agreements.[35]

Contemporaries perceived that there had been a massive increase in the inflow of overseas enterprises to Britain from November 1931 and that this was the direct result of protectionism.[36] Interviews between CIA officials and foreign firms indicated that their decisions were, in fact, generally motivated either by the tariff, the gold standard departure, or a combination of these factors.[37] More detailed information on the reasons given by individual firms is available from a database assembled by the authors, based on CIA files regarding 117 foreign companies that established British plants (hereafter the CIA database).[38] Surviving correspondence with individual firms did not always provide clear main reasons for their decision to commence UK production. However, in 28 cases the main reasons were discernible: 10 cited the new tariffs; 5 the gold standard departure; 12 mentioned both these factors; and the final firm emphasised adverse conditions in Germany.[39]

The September 1931 gold standard departure was clearly an important influence. It both raised the cost of supplying the British market by exports and reduced the foreign currency cost of acquiring British assets.[40] Earlier writers tend to discount the role of devaluation in stimulating recovery, seeing its trade impact as at best ephemeral.[41] Recent accounts suggest a much more positive role, although in Eichengreen's assessment mainly because breaking links with the gold standard 'freed up monetary and fiscal policies' so that '[n]o longer was it necessary to restrict domestic credit to defend convertibility'.[42] However, contemporary evidence suggests that depreciation had a further positive role, in stimulating fdi.

One of the most important inward investors during this period, Hoover, was unaffected by the tariff since it supplied the British market from Canada, thus enjoying imperial preference. However, depreciation, which Hoover claimed had increased their import costs by at least 15 per cent, led them to abandon an extension to their Canadian plant and build a UK factory instead, designed to supply Britain and act as a distribution centre for Europe and the Empire.[43] While it is probable that much of the competitive exchange advantage gained in 1931 was eroded during the following two years,[44] the inward direct investment it stimulated was unlikely to have been abandoned provided it continued to be profitable. The evidence presented in Table 1.4 indicates that despite the pound's subsequent recovery the vast majority of fdi generated during this period was still present at the end of 1936.

While depreciation was clearly a significant determinant of fdi, the tariff appears to have been of greater importance. A substantial proportion of companies mentioned only the tariff, while some required both the mutually-reinforcing tariff and depreciation effects. In other cases either influence was considered sufficient; as a representative of the Dutch embroidery firm J. Andriesse & Sons told the CIA, the gold standard departure led them to commence manufacture in Britain, 'but, of course, in case England would not have gone off the gold standard we should have been compelled to start in this country also because of the import duties'.[45]

Several firms which moved to Britain following the Emergency Tariff complained when they discovered that the General Tariff duties were lower than anticipated, one even claiming that it had 'been somewhat misled by the Government Offices and by the direct and indirect statements of the Press, when they tried to get manufacturers over to establish factories in this country'.[46] Nonetheless, devaluation and protection contributed to a dramatic fall in manufacturing imports. Between 1931 and 1932 Dutch and German exports to Britain both fell by 61 per cent, and those of Switzerland by 64 per cent. By late 1932, following the Ottawa agreements, 85 per cent of British imports from Germany were subject to duties, most at nominal rates of 11 per cent or more.[47]

The uneven incidence of tariffs had dramatic effects on some sectors. Germany had supplied virtually all British imports of artificial silk stockings, accounting for about a third of German output; duties of up to 75 per cent had brought appalling distress to the Chemnitz district. German delegates to the Anglo-German trade discussions in late 1932 alleged that specific duties on knitwear and scissors were equivalent to tariffs of 90 and 250 per cent respectively.[48] There were many instances where the value of imports from Germany during the first ten months of 1932 fell to only one-third or less of 1930 levels, including important groups such as silk or rayon fabrics (74 per cent fall), electrical products (69 per cent), artificial silk hosiery (80 per cent), semi-manufactured iron (91 per cent) and toys (70 per cent).[49] This obviously provided an extremely powerful inducement to jump tariff barriers by setting up UK production. Several continental governments tried to deter firms from doing so, using exchange controls, prohibitive export duties on second-hand machinery, or even obstructing the migration of key workers.[50] However, firms were often able to evade such restrictions.[51]

The character of firms attracted to Britain

Comparing fdi in the aftermath of the tariff with that during the 1920s presents a number of difficulties. There are no comprehensive employment figures for new multinationals prior to November 1931, though there are (imperfect) comparative data for the number and sectoral composition of new plants. Bostock and Jones have assembled the most comprehensive historical database of British inward fdi.[52] This indicates that during the 1920s an average of 16.7 new overseas firms per year established British plants, while the government data referred to earlier record 275 new foreign-owned plants during the eighteen months following the tariff. Analysis of a sample of 80 of these firms, for which the necessary details are available, indicates that 74 can be classified as fdi (being branches or subsidiaries of foreign enterprises or joint ventures).[53] The remaining six comprised firms or individuals undertaking wholesale transfers of production to Britain. If the sample is typical of the government data as a whole, around 92.5 per cent of the firms listed represented fdi; thus during the 18 months following the introduction of the Emergency Tariff the number of new multinationals averaged around 170 per year, about 10 times the average for the 1920s recorded in the Bostock and Jones database. However, given the preponderance of small factories the increase in employment arising from this fdi would not have been proportional.

The Bostock and Jones database lists only 20 new multinationals established during 1932, a fraction of the number indicated by the above figures. However, the nature of new entrants following the tariff makes them much more difficult to identify via a literature search method.[54] A large proportion were relatively small enterprises in industries not characterised by giant plants, which would therefore be much harder to identify as a result of their smaller size.[55] It could be argued that the Bostock and Jones database may also omit a considerable number of similar small firms during the 1920s. However, a CIA review of overseas-based plants established prior to the Emergency Tariff and a published study of the leather goods industry corroborates their evidence that there were extremely few earlier entrants in sectors such as clothing, textiles, and leather goods, where the smaller tariff-jumping enterprises of the early 1930s were concentrated.[56]

A sectoral comparison of firms moving to Britain from November 1931 and those arriving during the 1920s is also subject to difficulties. The published government data for the eighteen months following the Emergency Tariff (hereafter the government data) lists products manufactured by foreign firms, rather than the products produced by each firm, disaggregated by region and each quadrant of the London conurbation, at six-monthly intervals. Cross-referencing the government data with the CIA database enabled the identification of some firms initially unclassified; the remaining 26 unclassified firms represented 9.45 per cent of the 275 recorded. A comparison of the government data and the CIA database, which provides more detailed information for a smaller sample (117 firms) shows that in only one industry, textiles, is a large difference observed. The sectoral distribution of classified firms using the government and CIA data is compared with that of the Bostock and Jones database for the 1920s in Table 1.3. Post-tariff firms were concentrated in three long-established industries severely affected by the tariff: textiles, clothing & footwear, and leather goods, together with three more capital-intensive sectors that had witnessed heavy fdi during the 1920s, electrical equipment and chemicals (both partly covered by earlier tariffs) and other metal goods. Motor vehicles (which had received substantial protection since 1915) experienced negligible new fdi, in contrast to the 1920s.

A 1931 advert for Firestone tyres produced at their Great West Road factory, London.

The prevailing theory of multinational investment suggests that firms will only respond to tariffs by setting up production overseas if they have 'ownership advantages' over host-nation producers which can be transferred abroad.[57] In the absence of any firm-specific competitive advantage,

Table 1.3 Percentage distribution of classified firms in the government data and the CIA database*, compared with firms in the Bostock and Jones database for 1920–29

1980 UK SIC	Government	CIA	1920–1929
14 Mineral ore processing	0.00	0.00	1.80
16 Electricity supply	0.00	0.00	1.20
22 Metal manufacturing	1.61	0.75	3.59
24 Non-metallic mineral products	3.21	2.99	1.80
25 Chemicals	11.65	11.94	17.96
26 Man-made fibers	0.80	0.00	1.20
31 Other metal goods	8.43	6.72	10.18
32 Mechanical engineering	2.01	2.24	13.77
33 Office machinery	0.80	0.75	2.40
34 Electrical engineering	14.86	14.93	14.37
35 Motor vehicles & parts	0.00	0.75	5.39
36 Other transport equipment	0.40	0.00	1.80
37 Instrument engineering	4.82	5.22	2.99
41/2 Food, drink & tobacco	2.81	2.99	8.98
43 Textiles	16.06	23.13	0.00
44 Leather and leather goods	7.63	8.21	0.00
45 Clothing & footwear	12.05	10.45	2.40
46 Timber & wooden furniture	4.42	1.49	1.20
47 Paper and paper products	2.81	1.49	2.40
48 Rubber & plastics	1.61	2.99	4.79
49 Other manufacturing	4.02	2.99	1.80

Source: House of Commons, *Parliamentary Debates*, Vol. 266 (1932), cols 1331–34; Vol. 273 (1932), cols 734–37; Vol. 278 (1933), cols 917–19; CIA database; Bostock & Jones database.
Note:* Also includes firms in the Bostock & Jones database for 1932.

domestic producers should be better able to capture the benefits of local production than plants established by overseas firms.[58] The literature highlights two types of ownership advantage. The first type, widely considered the most important, involves their possession of proprietary intangible assets, created by investments in, and experience of, technological and marketing activities, together labelled 'product differentiation'. Such assets may also include special managerial skills and surplus entrepreneurial manpower. The second type involves the large size of multinationals, which partly captures product differentiation advantages, but also provides additional benefits such as access to capital markets, diversification of risk, superior information and greater political influence.[59]

Jones and Bostock's study of early US fdi in the UK indicated that US enterprises had substantial ownership advantages because of America's superiority in mass-production and science-based industries derived from Chandlerian three-pronged investment in manufacturing, marketing, and management.[60] US investment was concentrated in capital-intensive industries such as machinery, chemicals, branded foodstuffs and vehicles, in which America had a substantial technological lead and extensive managerial hierarchies were particularly important. The ownership advantages of American corporations, which dominated fdi during the 1920s, therefore appear to have been of both types.

However, during the immediate aftermath of the tariff fdi was dominated by continental European firms, which were generally of much smaller size than US multinationals. For example most German entrants were relatively small firms rather than the major German corporations. Their production was dominated by consumer goods, particularly branded products, in sectors where quality and design were of considerable importance. The first type of advantage, superiority in product differentiation, entrepreneurship and so on, could therefore be expected to dominate. The ownership advantages of such firms appear to have been considerable. A substantial number imported specialist 'niche' processes, hitherto unknown in the UK. For example the Hungarian firm P. Leiner & Co. established a plant for dyeing and curing sheep skins for use as furs, a process entirely new to Britain.[61] Similarly, Dutch cotton velour weavers Raymakers employed a process in their Accrington factory that was hitherto unused in Lancashire – involving the pile being cut in the loom – which affected the character of the finished fabric.[62] A number of other textile and hosiery firms imported processes which were not yet widely deployed in Britain, allowing them to manufacture different products to those of British industry, or to produce similar products more efficiently. Other firms produced 'speciality' products of their source country, such as Viennese knitwear.

Many of the new foreign-owned firms in the clothing, textiles and leather goods industries produced lines which faced little domestic competition as they aimed for the higher quality sections of their markets, which were largely neglected by British manufacturers. This neglect was intimately connected with Britain's failure to compete in terms of design. For example, a Belgian manufacturer of imitation hand embroidery produced by power machines told the CIA that, 'At one time . . . over 90 per cent of this trade had been in British hands, but for the last seven years rather less than 60 per cent had been supplied from home sources. The reason . . . was that the British manufacturer was mainly concerned with the bulk trade and would not bother about the finicky specialised goods . . . sold primarily on merits of design.'[63]

Detailed investigations during the mid-1930s by the government-appointed Council for Art and Industry highlighted serious deficiencies in British industrial design, relative to market requirements and continental production (particularly for higher-quality goods), for many of the sectors in which post-tariff fdi was concentrated.⁶⁴ The influence of the new entrants is illustrated by the example of leather goods. The British leather handbag market was dominated by German companies based in Offenbach, which were technically advanced and employed trained designers, or even professional artists.⁶⁵ Despite advances during and after the First World War, by 1931 the British industry was still notably less technically efficient and advanced than its German counterpart and had not yet begun to employ trained designers. The arrival of foreign firms (largely from Offenbach) during the early 1930s caused considerable 'heartburning' among established domestic producers.⁶⁶ Partly as a result of this competition, the industry achieved rapid design and technical advances during the 1930s. Design and production methods were imported to Britain by the overseas entrants partly through the transfer of key workers, skilled in the relevant techniques. As Table 1.1 shows, during the first year of the tariff overseas entrants imported some 615 key workers, allowed in by government under temporary permits to train British staff and assemble machinery.

A further group of firms gained their competitive advantage by mass-producing consumer durable and other goods which were generally manufactured in Britain on a craft production basis, and in which British industry consequently failed to serve the mass market. For example, the CIA was informed by the retailer Whiteleys that foreign firms reduced production costs:

> not by . . . using inferior material and labour but by being constantly alive to the possibilities of more and more improved machinery and methods of manufacture . . . Hoover's and Ford's, or . . . quite a small concern like Hooks . . . have brought the actual method of production to this country or have gone abroad and made a close study of it . . .⁶⁷

Industries in which the CIA files indicate that overseas-based entrants gained a competitive advantage from the introduction of mass production techniques included vacuum and carpet sweepers, clocks, spectacle frames, footwear, and wooden tools and heels. These typically involved relatively labour-intensive operations, in which mass production techniques could be applied with reasonable efficiency without requiring giant plants. One notable post-tariff multinational which introduced revolutionary mass-production technology was the Czech footwear manufacturer Thomas Bata. Bata had pioneered footwear mass-production via a semi-automatic conveyor system, after studying Ford's River Rouge plant. By the end of the 1920s the firm had begun to adopt a multinational strategy in response to rising European tariff walls.⁶⁸ Bata had taken steps to commence UK production by January 1932 due to increased costs arising from the 'tariff . . . in conjunction with depreciated exchange rate . . . [while] the Ottawa agreements have put firms manufacturing in Britain in a favourable position to export to the Empire . . .'[69] The Bata factory, on a 600 acre site at East Tilbury, soon constituted a major competitor to established UK shoe manufacturers.[70]

Technology imports by British firms

In addition to stimulating fdi the 1931 tariff also led a number of British firms to take advantage of protection by importing foreign technology. While the reduction in overseas competition arising from the tariff might have been expected to have reduced pressure for technical change, the CIA papers and other contemporary evidence suggest that the tariff actually provided a substantial stimulus to technology imports, at least in some sectors, by reducing the perceived risk associated with costly investment. This is illustrated by the example of hosiery. Many companies, both foreign and British, sought to import fully-fashioned hosiery machines (together with key staff) following the tariff, British hosiery firms having hitherto generally confined investment to the cheaper circular machines.[71]

Fully-fashioned machines cost about £2,000 each, compared to around £150 for circular machines.[72] While it was generally accepted that they were much more efficient than their circular counterparts, the presence of well-established overseas competitors, paying significantly lower wages, had previously inhibited firms from making the heavy investment entailed in their purchase (despite the fact that they were a labour-saving technology which should, therefore, have been more suitable for Britain's high labour cost conditions).[73] Fully-fashioned machines proved extremely successful; the widespread conversion to this technology by British firms (together with tariff protection, an expansion of domestic demand, and the establishment of overseas-based enterprises) resulted in a rise in employment in this section of the industry from 2,000 in 1930 to over 10,000 in 1939.[74] In addition to lowering risk, protectionism also reduced costs, by creating a supply of low-cost 'second-hand' machinery which had been made surplus to overseas capacity by the tariff.

Several British companies sought to copy foreign production methods by purchasing entire factories and shipping them to Britain 'lock, stock and barrel' (together with key staff), in order to introduce new processes in British industries such as silk velvet and wallpaper manufacture.[75] The tariff also led a number of British firms to form joint ventures with overseas suppliers. For example, the radio manufacturer Ekco began manufacturing bakelite radio cabinets, previously purchased from A.E.G. of Berlin (who had developed a process for manufacturing large bakelite mouldings of a size not produced in Britain), receiving assistance from A.E.G. in return for a fee and royalty. This allowed Ekco both to introduce its famous range of circular radios and to manufacture a wide variety of bakelite products for other companies, pioneering the introduction of this technology to Britain.[76]

The CIA files provide information on 19 British companies that imported technology either for their own use, or through joint ventures in which they appear to have been the dominant partner. Their sectoral distribution broadly reflected that of new foreign-based enterprises, suggesting that technology imports offered an alternative to fdi as a means of transmitting ownership advantages. However, available evidence suggests that such transfers were much less important than those via fdi. A December 1932 *Business* article claimed that British enterprises had only managed to start about a dozen factories to make goods that had formerly been imported, and the majority of these should have opened earlier in order to have secured markets before foreign firms established UK production.[77]

While the available evidence is far from perfect, it appears that British industry was generally slow to grasp the opportunities offered by the tariff and gold standard departure to move into markets previously served from abroad. The main entrepreneurial response appears to have come from foreign, rather than domestic, producers. This may reflect the inadequacy of patenting agreements and importing machinery and key staff as a means of transferring the ownership advantages possessed by foreign firms, or a lack of knowledge of the newly-available markets (or even a lack of entrepreneurship) on the part of British industry.

The economic impact of fdi

Britain's limited tariff protection during the 1920s led to the establishment, or expansion, of a substantial number of large foreign-controlled enterprises that played an important role in the long-term development of major British industries such as automobiles, tyres, and electrical engineering.[78] The firms moving to Britain following the events of Autumn 1931 were generally smaller concerns, operating in a wider variety of industries which were typically not as 'high-tech' as those which had dominated inward fdi during the previous decade. Nevertheless, these firms collectively provided a variety of both short and long-term benefits to the British economy.

By the end of April 1933 employment in the new foreign plants had reached almost 11,000, while it was estimated by their promoters that this would rise to over 17,000 when the factories were fully occupied.[79] Meanwhile aggregate UK-insured manufacturing employment had increased over the two years from the middle of 1931 by 275,000. Data, reproduced in Table 1.4, is available regarding the survival and employment growth of

Table 1.4 Employment in foreign plants established during 1932–1935 in 1936

Year	For initial year of establishment			For firms surviving to 1936	
	New factories	Employment*	Factories	Initial employment*	Employment in 1936
1932	140	8,500	120	6,600	12,300
1933	33	1,900	31	1,800	4,400
1934	34	2,300	28	2,100	2,800
1935	17	1,500	17	1,500	1,700

Source: Board of Trade, *Survey of Industrial Development, 1936* (London: HMSO, 1937), p. 8.

Notes: * Employment at the end of the year in which the factories were established.
N.B. this table includes both fdi and other enterprises of foreign origin and refers only to firms employing 25 or more people in December of their year of establishment.

foreign firms (with an initial employment of 25 or more) established from 1932–35, at the end of 1936. This indicates that only 14.3 per cent of foreign plants established during 1932 had closed by the end of 1936 (a high survival rate for new plants during this period).[80] Surviving plants had increased their employment by 86.4 per cent since the end of 1932, while aggregate employment in all such plants established in 1932 had risen by 44.7 per cent. Crowding out of employment that would otherwise have been provided by British-based firms appears to have been insubstantial, given that these firms were concentrated in sectors experiencing little direct competition from UK enterprises.[81]

The firms also assisted Britain's balance of payments by diverting production to Britain. According to an estimate based on 57 firms in the CIA database,[82] the 254 firms established following the tariff and still in existence in April 1933 diverted UK turnover very roughly estimated at £6.46 million, in addition to exports conducted from Britain (which were expected to be substantial).

The employment and balance of payments benefits were of much less economic importance, however, than the long-term diffusion of the 'ownership advantages' of these new enterprises to British industry. The CIA conducted detailed investigations of the expected net economic benefit of each firm; these indicate that many applicants offered significant advantages to British industry in areas such as technology, the organisation of production, design, and product diversification.[83] Similarly, investigations regarding overseas multinationals in Britain conducted by the TUC during the 1930s indicated that they were substantially more advanced than British firms in the use of mass production techniques.[84] Jones has noted that interwar multinationals transmitted a range of benefits to British industry, diffusing both superior technology and managerial and entrepreneurial skills (though he argues that these were not always

Model A Ford of the type produced at Trafford Park (car driven by John Rooth at Hastings Carnival, 1950).

appropriate for British conditions).[85] According to Law, this diffusion had a significant influence on the long-term industrial development of the South East (where interwar multinationals were strongly concentrated):

> many introduced new industries . . . and . . . reinforced that region's capacity for innovation. At the same time many of these firms needed materials and industrial services which stimulated these other activities in the London region. Finally, many . . . introduced new production and management processes which diffused to other firms in the region and gave valuable new experience to potential entrepreneurs who later established their own firms . . .[86]

This is corroborated by Smithies' study of inter-war Luton, which emphasised the demonstration effect to local businessmen of Vauxhall's plant layout and production line techniques, as well as the plant organisation and personnel management systems of Electrolux and Skefco.[87]

Evidence from the CIA files confirms the importance of overseas firms as agents of innovation in a range of sectors including leather goods, hosiery and a variety of other textile products, fashion clothing, and a diverse group of light assembly industries such as footwear, vacuum cleaners, spectacle frames, and clocks. While the literature on multinationals and technology transfer in a developing country context has highlighted problems of 'enclave' investment and the crowding-out of domestic research capacity, Britain's cultural and technological proximity to the source countries, together with the relatively small size of most 'multinationals' compared to their post-war counterparts, acted to minimise such effects. At a time when protection might otherwise have reduced pressures for innovation, the establishment of overseas enterprises went some way towards maintaining competition and provided an example to British industry of what could be achieved using foreign production, design, and managerial techniques.

Conclusion

The scope of British tariff legislation had a major influence on the level and composition of inward-fdi throughout the interwar period. During the 1920s tariffs had been applied principally to capital-intensive, 'high-tech' industries such as automobiles and components, tyres, chemicals, and artificial silk, stimulating substantial direct investment in these sectors by major overseas (mainly American) corporations. The extension of protection from November 1931 stimulated fdi by a much larger number of smaller, specialist, more labour-intensive (mainly continental) firms in sectors such as textiles, clothing, leather goods and electrical engineering. These were industries in which a superiority in design or production technology gave overseas firms substantial advantages over British concerns, but in which such advantages could often be realised without multidivisional corporate organisation.

Although the impact of protectionism in Britain has long been a source of controversy, recent research has tended to indicate that it was an appropriate second-best strategy given the distorted, protectionist, world trading system of the 1930s. Studies by Foreman-Peck, Hatton, and Kitson and Solomou have indicated that (contrary to earlier studies) protection had a favourable macroeconomic impact.[88] Meanwhile, in the light of the price behaviour of firms, the inflationary effects were minimal.[89] While the contribution of fdi to this process was probably of relatively minor importance, it does indicate one avenue by which the positive effects noted in these aggregate studies were realised.

The main economic benefits of fdi were, however, considerably longer-term in nature. Overseas-based firms diversified production in a range of important industries, opening up new markets and introducing new products, processes, and design standards. The extent to which such intangible factors were transmitted to, and benefited, British industry is, by their nature, very difficult to quantify. However, the evidence reviewed above corroborates previous studies suggesting that these effects were positive and significant. In the context of a world rapidly moving towards protected trading blocs, Britain's combination of protectionism with liberal access to incoming overseas enterprises allowed it to capture some of the economic gains offered by overseas production techniques that would otherwise have been lost as tariff walls priced foreign suppliers out of British markets.

Notes

* We would like to thank Colin Jennings, Geoffrey Jones, Paul Walker and the participants at a session of the 1998 Economic History Society Conference for their comments on earlier versions of this article, and Oliver White for help regarding the motor industry. We also gratefully acknowledge the assistance of the ESRC Data Archive, Modern Records Centre, Nottinghamshire Local Studies Library, Public Record Office, and Slough Estates Archive. Any errors or omissions are, of course, our own.

1 G. Jones, 'Foreign multinationals and British industry before 1945', *Economic History Review*, 2nd ser., XLI (1988), 429–53, p. 438.

2 A. Hagen, 'German direct investment in the UK, 1871–1918', *Business History*, 41 (1999), 37–68, p. 50. The company, which was dissatisfied with the operation of its London plant, closed it down when the British government lowered the duties on manufactured chocolates in 1913.

3 Hagen, 'German direct investment', p. 50.

4 J. H. Dunning, *American Investment in British Manufacturing Industry* (London: Allen & Unwin, 1958), p. 33; Jones, 'Foreign multinationals', p. 439; P. Hertner, 'German multinational enterprise before 1914: some case studies', in P. Hertner and G. Jones (eds.), *Multinationals: Theory and History* (Aldershot: Gower, 1986), p. 124; A. Hagen, 'Export versus direct investment in the German optical industry: Carl Zeiss, Jena and Glaswerk Schott & Gen. in the UK, from their beginnings to 1933', *Business History*, 38 (1996), pp. 1–20. A. Hagen, 'German FDI in the British chemical industry to 1914', paper presented to European Business History Association Conference, Göteborg, 30 Aug. – 1 Sept. 1996. With regard to Germany, Hagen emphasises that this was only one factor, and both she and Hertner note that the incentive was subsequently weakened by lax judicial interpretation of the law.

5 Hagen, 'German direct investment', pp. 50–51.

6 G. Jones, *The Evolution of International Business: An Introduction* (London: Routledge, 1996), p. 121; J. A. Brander and B. J. Spencer, 'Foreign direct investment with unemployment and endogenous taxes and tariffs', *Journal of International Economics*, 22 (1987), pp. 257–79; T. A. B. Corley, 'The nature of multinationals, 1870–1939', pp. 43–56 in A. Teichova, M. Levy-Leboyer and H. Nussbaum (eds), *Historical Studies in International Corporate Business* (Cambridge: CUP, 1989); I. J. Horstmann and J. R. Markusen, 'Strategic investments and the development of multinationals', *International Economic Review* 28 (1987), pp. 109–21; Mira Wilkins, *The Maturing of Multinational Enterprise: American Business Abroad from 1914 to 1970* (Cambridge, Mass.: Harvard University Press, 1974).

7 F. Capie, *Depression and Protectionism: Britain between the Wars* (London: Allen & Unwin, 1983), p. 44.

8 G. Jones et al., *Impact of Foreign Multi-National Investment in Britain since 1850* [computer file], Colchester: ESRC Data Archive, 1993; F. Bostock and

G. Jones, 'Foreign multinationals in British manufacturing, 1850–1962', *Business History* 36 (1994), pp. 89–126; G. Jones and F. Bostock, 'US multinationals in British manufacturing before 1962', *Business History Review*, 70 (1996), pp. 67–116. There are slight differences in the number of firms given in these sources, due to revisions of the database.

9 Jones, 'Foreign multinationals', p. 439; M. J. French, 'The emergence of a U.S. multinationalenterprise: the Goodyear Tire and Rubber Company, 1910–39', *Economic History Review* XL (1987), pp. 64–79; A. Plummer, *New British Industries in the Twentieth Century* (London: Pitman, 1937), p. 84. However, the Dyestuffs Act, aimed at protecting an industry enormously expanded during the war when German supplies were cut off, does not appear to have led to inward investment: 'The Germans . . . seem to have decided that it would bring more hostility than profit', W. J. Reader, *Imperial Chemical Industries: A History. Vol. I, The Forerunners 1870–1926* (London: Oxford University Press, 1970), p. 440.

10 Slough Estate Archive, press cuttings book, 'The work-hard-and-be-happy town of Slough', *Evening News* (13 February 1929).

11 D. C. Coleman, *Courtaulds: An Economic and Social History* (Oxford: Clarendon, 1969), pp. 265–66.

12 *The Times*, 5 January 1928, p. 22. He subsequently set up production in Bradford.

13 Nottinghamshire Local Studies Library, press cuttings file, 'New silk mill for Nottingham', *Nottingham Guardian* (6 March 1928). It is not clear whether this factory was, in fact, subsequently opened.

14 Dunning, 'Growth of U.S. investment', p. 258; M. Wilkins and F. E. Hill, *American Business Abroad: Ford on Six Continents* (Detroit: Wayne State University Press, 1964), pp. 46–7, 102, 111–12, & 134.

15 Alfred P. Sloan, *My Years with General Motors* (New York: Doubleday, 1964), pp. 318–321. Sloan also pointed out the British system of taxation, based on the bore of the cylinder, penalised the characteristically large bore and short stroke American engines (the Ford AF model, illustrated, used a small-bore engine of 14.9 h.p. designed specifically for the British market to beat the horsepower tax).

16 Public Record Office (hereafter, PRO), BT55/84, extract from *The National Union of Manufacturers Journal*, October 1925.

17 PRO, BT55/84, review of firms established in UK following the McKenna duties, n. d., c.1928. Fiat, for example, planned to import engines but otherwise the rest of the vehicles, including bodies, tyres, batteries, lighting and springs, were to be British made. Willis Overland Crossley, on the other hand, used an 1802 cc Morris Oxford engine.

18 PRO, BT55/84, review of tyre factories established since the imposition of tariffs, n. d., c.1928; French, 'Goodyear', pp. 62–75; J. Marshall, *The History of the Great West Road: Its Social and Economic Influence on the Surrounding Area* (Hounslow: Heritage Publications, 1995), p. 54.

19 PRO, BT55/84, extract from *Morning Post*, 20 October 1930.

20 J. M. Stopford and L. Turner, *Britain and the Multinationals* (Chichester: Wiley, 1985), p. 60.

21 *West Herts. Press* (May 1929), reproduced in T. Paish et al., *The Book of Watford* (Watford: Pageprint, 1987), p. 174.

22 PRO, BT56/47/CIA2146, note, 22 January 1932; BT56/48/CIA2184, note, 4 February 1932; J. Armstrong, 'International influences on the development of London business: the case of the Park Royal industrial estate between the wars', unpublished typescript, p. 11; Dunning, *American Investment*, p. 32.

23 Capie, *Depression*; National Institute of Economic and Social Research, *Trade Regulations and Commercial Policy of the United Kingdom* (Cambridge: CUP, 1943), pp. 21–2.

24 T. Rooth, *British Protectionism and the International Economy* (Cambridge: CUP, 1993), pp. 63–70, discusses the manoeuvres involved.

25 *The Times*, 11 May 1932, p. 8.

26 These are nominal tariffs; effective levels of protection were normally higher. For estimates see Capie, *Depression*; M. Kitson, S. Solomou and M. Weale, 'Effective protection and economic recovery in the United Kingdom during the 1930s', *Economic History Review*, XLIV (1991), pp. 328–38.

27 H. Hutchinson, *Tariff-Making and Industrial Reconstruction: An Account of the Work of the Import Duties Advisory Committee 1932–39* (London: Harrap, 1965), pp. 45–7.

28 PRO, BT56/40/CIA1800/71, memorandum by Horace Wilson, 19 December 1931.

29 PRO, BT56/40/CIA1800/71, 'Establishment of foreign factories in this country', 14 April 1932.

30 No data was provided after October 1932; for some countries figures are given for only one period, presumably due to the small number of firms in the remaining six months.

31 Estimated using CIA database.

32 E. W. Pasold, *Ladybird Ladybird: A Story of Private Enterprise* (Manchester: Manchester University Press, 1977), p. 274.

33 Wilkins, *Maturing*, p. 171. However the tariff may still have influenced the *level* of US fdi, acting as an important counter-balance to pressure which existing American companies faced to close their British plants, at a time when many were experiencing considerable financial difficulties; see Dunning, *American Investment*, p. 45.

34 Wilkins, *Maturing*, p. 172.

35 Jones, *Evolution*, p. 41.

36 C. Challen, 'These new competitors – are they affecting your business?', *Business* (December 1932), pp. 9–10; Modern Records Centre, Warwick, Trades Union Congress papers, MSS. 29/103.3/1, Trades Union General Council memorandum, 'Conditions of workers employed by foreign firms established in this country', 11 January 1935; D. H. Smith, *The Industries of Greater London* (London: P. S. King, 1933), p. 164.

37 PRO, BT56/40/CIA1800/71, 'Establishment of foreign firms in this country', memorandum,14 April 1932.

38 The CIA database, together with a database compiled from the more comprehensive, but less detailed, government data, are available on request from the ESRC Data Archive, Colchester.

39 Economic and political instability in Germany led a number of German businessmen to consider migration even prior to the rise of the Hitler government. However, the CIA database indicates that only around 12 per cent of German-based enterprises (for which this information was available) were 'migrant' firms in that their overseas parent was immediately closed down (some additional firms indicated that they might terminate German production when their British plants became well-established).

40 The role of exchange rate depreciation in stimulating fdi, via wealth effects, is discussed in K. A. Froot and J. C. Stein, 'Exchange rates and foreign direct investment: an imperfect capital markets approach', *Quarterly Journal of Economics*,

106 (1991), pp. 1191–1217. More generally, given the growth of controls on capital flows during the 1930s, together with the less globally integrated nature of financial markets, the main economic arguments against exchange rate changes influencing fdi, which assume perfect capital markets, are not valid for this period.

41 D. H. Aldcroft, *The Inter-war Economy: Britain, 1919–1939* (London: Batsford, 1970), p. 281; W. A. Lewis, *Economic Survey, 1919–1939* (London: Allen & Unwin, 1949), p. 82, cited in Capie, *Protection*, p. 134.

42 B. Eichengreen, *Golden Fetters: The Gold Standard and the Great Depression 1919–1939* (Oxford: Oxford University Press, 1992), p. 21. See also S. Solomou, *Themes in Macroeconomic History: The UK Economy, 1919–1939* (Cambridge: CUP, 1996); P. Temin, *Lessons from the Great Depression* (Cambridge, Mass.: MIT Press, 1989), pp. 74–6.

43 *The Times*, 20 January 1932, p. 10.

44 J. Redmond, 'An indicator of the effective exchange rate of the pound in the nineteen-thirties', *Economic History Review*, XXXIII (1980), pp. 83–91. However, M. Kitson and S. Solomou, *Protectionism and Economic Revival: the British Interwar Economy* (Cambridge: CUP, 1990), pp. 45–9, suggest that export competitiveness may not have been completely eroded until 1937, and that import competitiveness, enhanced by tariffs, was more enduring.

45 PRO, BT56/49/CIA2277, note dated 4 July 1932.

46 PRO, BT56/40/CIA1800/72, letter from Peltzer-Lister Velvet Co., 5 May 1932.

47 *Economist*, Ottawa Supplement, 22 October 1932.

48 PRO, BT11/189, note of meeting, 7 December 1932.

49 PRO, BT11/189. Some of the examples cover the first nine months.

50 *The Times*, 11 March 1932, p. 13, and 31 March 1932, p. 11; PRO, BT56/40/CIA1800/71, BT56/47/CIA2169, BT56/40/CIA1800/102, BT56/50/CIA2347.

51 PRO, BT56/48/CIA2184, note, 4 Feb. 1932; Pasold, *Ladybird, Ladybird*, pp. 294–5 & 387–8.

52 Jones et al, *Impact*; Bostock and Jones, 'Foreign multinationals'; Jones and Bostock, 'US multinationals'.

53 Source: CIA database.

54 This formed the major data source for non-US firms in the Bostock and Jones database, see Jones et al., *Impact*.

55 Overseas-based enterprises establishing production in Britain in the aftermath of the tariff employed an average of 42.8 British workers at the end of April 1933. By comparison, according to a contemporary estimate, by 1932 the 197 US manufacturing plants in Britain employed an average of 336.9 workers each – see Dunning, *American Investment*, p. 44.

56 PRO, BT56/1800, 'Notes on foreign firms established in the United Kingdom', 5 June 1931; J. W. Waterer, *Leather in Life, Art and Industry* (London: Faber & Faber, 1946).

57 There is an alternative theoretical approach to multinationals, based on transactions costs.

58 R. McCulloch, 'New perspectives of foreign direct investment', pp. 37–53 in K. A. Froot (ed) *Foreign Direct Investment* (Chicago: University of Chicago Press, 1993), p. 43; S. Lall, *Multinationals, Technology and Exports* (Basingstoke: Macmillan, 1985), p. 7.

59 Lall, *Multinationals*, pp. 2–3.

60 Jones and Bostock, 'US multinationals', p. 79.

61 PRO, BT56/50/CIA2359, letter from Leiner's representative, 4 April 1932.
62 PRO, BT56/46/CIA2059, letter from Storey, 2 February 1932.
63 PRO, BT56/47/CIA2112, note dated 8 January 1932.
64 PRO, BT57/1–35.
65 Waterer, *Leather*, p. 225.
66 Waterer, *Leather*, p. 226.
67 PRO, BT 56/40/CIA1800/68.
68 A. Cekota, *Entrepreneur Extraordinary: The Biography of Thomas Bata* (Rome: EIS, 1968).
69 *The Times*, 24 January 1933, p. 19.
70 A. Fox, *The History of the National Union of Boot and Shoe Operatives 1874– 1957* (Oxford: Blackwell, 1958).
71 PRO, BT56/47/CIA2159, note dated 18 January 1932.
72 PRO, BT56/47/CIA2142, note dated 19 January 1932.
73 PRO, BT56/47/CIA2163, letter from R. Allard, 12 May 1932.
74 Board of Trade, *Board of Trade Working Party Report: Hosiery* (London: HMSO, 1946), p. 11.
75 PRO, BT56/50/CIA2338, letter, 22 February 1932; PRO BT56/50/CIA2302, letter from Ashley Wallpaper Co., 9 February 1932.
76 K. Geddes and G. Bussey, *The Setmakers: A History of the Radio and Television Industry* (London: Brema, 1991), pp. 114–32.
77 Challen, 'New competitors'.
78 Jones, 'Foreign multinationals', pp. 431–35.
79 House of Commons, *Parliamentary Debates*, Vol. 278 (1933), col. 918.
80 See G. R. Allen, 'The growth of industry on trading estates, 1920–39, with special reference to Slough Trading Estate', *Oxford Economic Papers*, 3 (1951), pp. 272–300.
81 See P. Scott and T. Rooth, 'Public policy and foreign-based enterprises in Britain prior to the Second World War', *Historical Journal*, 42 (1999), pp. 495–515.
82 This figure is likely to be a conservative estimate, as firms providing turnover data had a lower average initial employment than other firms on the CIA database.
83 Scott and Rooth, 'Public policy.'
84 P. Scott, 'The wolf at the door: the trade union movement and overseas multinationals in Britain during the 1930s', *Social History*, 23 (1998), pp. 195–210.
85 Jones, 'Foreign multinationals', pp. 439–42.
86 C. M. Law, *British Regional Development Since World War 1* (London: David & Charles, 1980), p. 177.
87 E. D. Smithies, 'The contrast between north and south in England 1918–1939: a study of economic, social and political problems with particular reference to the experience of Burnley, Halifax, Ipswich, and Luton' (unpublished Ph.D. thesis, University of Leeds, 1974), p. 65.
88 J. Foreman-Peck, 'The British tariff and industrial protection in the 1930s: an alternative model', *Economic History Review*, xxxiv (1981), pp. 132–39; T. J. Hatton, 'Perspectives on the economic recovery of the 1930s', *Royal Bank of Scotland Review*, 158 (1988), pp. 18–32; Kitson and Solomou, *Protectionism*.
89 Solomou, *Themes*, pp. 142–45.

"Protectionism and the growth of overseas multinational enterprise in interwar Britain"

A retrospective

Peter Scott

This article formed part of a larger project, examining the interrelationships between government policy, inward foreign direct investment (hereafter fdi), and British industrial development, during the period of high international tariff barriers from 1914 to the 1960s (jointly with my colleague at the University of Portsmouth Tim Rooth, who sadly passed away in 2017).[1] The broad aim of the project was to examine the impacts of British tariffs and other measures of trade protection (such as Imperial Preference and "Buy British" campaigns) on inward fdi and related phenomena – firm relocations to Britain and tariff-induced technology transfer initiatives.

The research was facilitated by the then recently-completed Bostock and Jones dataset on multinational investment in Britain since 1850.[2] This was supplemented by papers in The National Archives – mainly in the T (Treasury); BT (Board of Trade), and CIA (Board of Trade, Office of the Chief Industrial Advisor) classes – and the Bank of England Archive, together with a broad range of other primary and secondary sources.

Neoclassical economic theory implies that tariffs damage the countries that impose them. However, this is based on simplistic assumptions that ignore dynamic effects such as tariff-jumping foreign direct investment and the resulting diffusion of international best practice, in both "hard" technology and less tangible knowledge such as superior management and marketing systems. The project showed that tariffs and other protectionist measures played important roles in the development of both "new" industries, such as the automobile, electrical, and machinery sectors, together with a range of other industries with process and/or product technologies that had not hitherto been widely applied in Britain.

Moreover, such advantages proved "persistent" with tariff-jumping companies often retaining a presence in Britain long after the barriers that had led to their initial investments had ceased to be important. Such effects significantly modify the predictions of neoclassical trade theory, which assumes a world of perfect information and zero transactions costs and thereby greatly underestimates the benefits of tariff-induced fdi, while exaggerating the long-term costs.

However, generalising the findings of this project to the twenty-first century is problematic. During the early and middle decades of the twentieth century inward direct investment in Britain provided preferential access not only to the UK, but to the Empire and, later, the sterling area. Then in the last quarter of the twentieth century Britain's EU membership, in conjunction with its status as the only major English-speaking EU nation, were important factors behind inward fdi by automobile and electronics firms from Japan and South-east Asia. However, following its EU departure, the attractions of Britain as a host nation for multinationals, and the resulting technological, employment, and other benefits flowing from this, have been considerably weakened. Moreover, in a globalised world of low trade barriers, the advantages of market-seeking fdi have become progressively unimportant compared to cost-reducing and strategic motives.

Notes

1 The other outputs included: Peter Scott, 'The location of early overseas multinationals in Britain, 1900–1939: patterns and determinants,' *Regional Studies,* 32, 6, (1998), 489–502; Peter Scott and Tim Rooth, 'Public policy and foreign-based enterprises in Britain prior to the Second World War,' *The Historical Journal*, 42, 2, (1999), 495–515; Tim Rooth and Peter Scott, 'British public policy and inward direct investment during the "dollar gap" era,' *Enterprise & Society*, 3, 1, (2002), 124–61.
2 Francis Bostock and Geoffrey Jones, 'Impact of foreign mult-national investment since 1850,' UK Data Service, SN 3142, 1994, http://doi.org/10.5255/UKDA-SN-3142-1

2 The making of the First Czechoslovak Republic and the national control of companies

The nostrification policy and economic nationalism, 1918–1938*

Patrick Crowhurst

The First Czechoslovak Republic was created on 28 October 1918 in the face of determined Austrian opposition.[1] The declaration was made twelve days after the Emperor Charles had offered Czechs autonomy in his manifesto 'To my loyal Austrian people' and after the Social Democrats had twice invited other national groups to discuss the possibility of a democratic federation of national states.[2] For the Czechs the new republic represented a return to the historic kingdom of Bohemia: a powerful and prestigious former Czech state.[3] Czechs also saw it as compensation for their defeat in 1620 at the Battle of the White Mountain, which had been followed by three hundred years of Habsburg rule. It was also a product of the intense Czech nationalism that had grown during the First World War, when Czechs had joined the French and Italian armies and fought against Germany and Austria–Hungary. For the Austrians, Czechoslovakia represented a denial of the normal state of affairs in which the German-speaking peoples had dominated Central Europe.[4] The elevation of the Czechs to be the rulers of the new state rankled. Austrians were bitterly disappointed that national self-determination, given to the Czechs and Slovaks, should be denied to them.[5] They also pointed to earlier declarations of loyalty by Masaryk and Beneš to the Habsburgs and argued that the Czechs should have been given self-government within the Empire and not a separate state. Each group felt that they had justice on their side, but Czechs, who formed a majority in the new country, moved quickly to establish a government, new currency and their own effective power.[6] Czechs therefore introduced their 'nostrification' policy, designed to transfer ownership of all economic activities (banks, manufacturing industry and business) from Austrian to Czech control, because they considered that they could not rely on the loyalty of the Austrians in the new Czechoslovakia.

However, nostrification, though justified in Czech eyes, was not likely to achieve the results the government wanted. It made it more difficult for companies to compete in the new conditions created by the new economic nationalism of Central and Eastern Europe. Why this was so, and what the results were, is the subject of this paper. Three case studies of different types of Czechoslovak company reveal how far the policy of 'nostrification' succeeded.

The making of the First Czechoslovak Republic

During the First World War, Germany had promised increased political power to the Austrians at the expense of the Czechs. The proclamation by the Národní Vbor of the independence of the Czechoslovak state on 28 October 1918 was fiercely contested by all German speakers.[7] Soon afterwards, a national government was established with the task of creating the new state of Czechs, Austrians, Slovaks, Poles and Ruthenes. The Czechs always maintained that they intended from the start to treat all national groups equally, but German groups boycotted the discussions.[8] In March 1919, Austrians demonstrated in Vienna against what they saw as high-handed Czech attitudes under the banner 'Nieder mit der tschechischen Tyrannei'.[9] This did not stop the government creating new institutions and administration for the fledgling state. It also set out to discover what assets the state possessed, so that a rational economic policy could be developed. Given the attitude of Germany and Austria, it is not surprising that the government decided that it was essential that these assets should be under the control of Czechoslovak citizens – the 'nostrification' policy.

The 'nostrification' policy

This was the transfer of foreign capital holdings from Austria and Germany to Czechoslovakia, a process aided by powerful financial groups in the USA, Britain, France and Belgium.[10] The attraction for foreign investors was the relatively high concentration of banking and industry, the relatively low level of wages, the political stability of the new state and its geographical position. This inflow of foreign capital enabled the government to order that companies should move their head offices from Vienna to Czechoslovakia. The policy also decreed that effective control of the capital, and thus of the management of the companies, should be controlled by Czechoslovak citizens. They should form a majority of the membership of the supervisory board (Verwaltungsrat) and additional shares would be in the hands of Czechoslovak banks. It was hoped in this way that the Czechoslovak economy would be managed by people who had demonstrated their loyalty to the new state by becoming citizens of it. Czechoslovak citizenship was granted on the basis of birth, residence and ownership of property, but it was not compulsory to be a Czechoslovak citizen in order to live in Czechoslovakia.

Autarky

This Czechoslovak 'nostrification' policy helped to provoke a response from the other Succession states. The early decision to impose tariffs on imported textiles was intended to protect the home industry. This had not been necessary under the old regime, because the different parts of the empire had specialised in agriculture, mining or industry and had exchanged their products under a low tariff system. Once the new states were created, everything changed. Each country wanted to become self-sufficient. Czechoslovakia, a mining and industrial state that had imported large quantities of food, imposed tariffs on foreign agricultural goods to try and support and develop its own agriculture. Agricultural states such as Hungary and Romania imposed tariffs on Czechoslovak machinery and bought from other countries such as Britain to develop their industrial base. The policy was only developed slowly – Poland and Hungary were both initially disrupted by war – and reached its peak during the early-1930s Depression. Mutual disagreements between the new states over frontiers and minority groups (Poles, Hungarians and Ruthenes in Czechoslovakia, Hungarians in Romania, Ukrainians in Poland) fuelled nationalist dislike of other states. What makes the Czechoslovak situation different was that it was driven mainly by a desire to seize economic power from a formerly dominant racial group, rather than build up its economic power.

Banks

Control of the banks was a key factor in establishing the new state. The former Habsburg government had centralised banking in Vienna and companies had used these banks as the main sources of finance. By 1919, a large Czech bank had also been established in Prague, the Iivnostenská Bank, and it had sufficient funds to buy control of the Böhmische Eskomte Bank. This in turn took over branches of the Kreditanstalt für Handel und Gewerbe and branches of other banks were given the choice of forming new Czechoslovak banks or amalgamating with existing ones.

The Viennese Merkur Bank became the Komerèní banka, branches of the Oesterreichische Länderbank joined the Hospodáàská Úvérní banka; the Wiener Bank Verein created a separate bank and the branches of the Verkehrsbank joined the Moravská agrární a prùmyslová banka. Branches of the

Anglo-Austrian Bank were amalgamated with the new Anglo-Czechoslo-vak Bank. This created a Czechoslovak banking system and confidence in the new banks. Firms were able to transfer their funds and head offices from Vienna to Czechoslovakia and became Czechoslovak.

Companies

While the banking system was being transformed, the government also car-ried out a detailed survey of Czechoslovak economic assets. A survey was made of all firms asking for detailed information about the number and value of shares, money, land, buildings, machinery, stocks of finished and part finished products, raw materials, vehicles, horses and any other assets and liabilities. These valuable documents formed the basis for all future government policies on industry, commerce and taxation. Without this sur-vey, it would have been impossible to formulate any policy, since the only data that had already been collected was in Vienna.

The next step was to try and transform them into Czechoslovak firms. This was more difficult. Many of the entrepreneurs who had established these companies were Viennese and still lived there at the end of the First World War. Their head offices, which were also the central office for sales and distribution, were also in Vienna. Following an agreement with the Austrian government in 1920, which cancelled the liquidation tax, all com-panies with factories in Czechoslovakia became Czechoslovak as did the branches of foreign companies that carried on business in the republic.

Transfer of companies to Czechoslovak citizenship

The next step was to try and bring these companies under the control of Czechoslovak citizens through what was termed the 'nostrification' law. As noted above, this stated that a majority of the board of directors had to be Czechoslovak citizens and live in the state. The Treaty of St Germain had laid down conditions for establishing citizenship in Czechoslovakia and other successor states. Article 70 stated that all who had the right to live in the former Austro-Hungarian monarchy (i.e., they had *Heimatrecht* or *pertinenza,* as it was called in the treaty) would be covered by the arti-cles.[11] Article 77 covered Czechs and Slovaks speaking their own language who had been born and lived all their lives in the area that now formed the Republic. These applied for Czechoslovak citizenship. So too did those Czechs who had adopted the German language and culture as a way of mak-ing a career in the Habsburg civil service or industry, but who still thought of themselves as Czechs. More complicated was the case of Austrians, many of whom never came to terms with the loss of Austrian dominance. These were covered by Article 78.[12] They had the right to choose which state they wanted to live in and had twelve months to make their choice. At the end of that time, if they did not choose to become citizens of the Czechoslovak state they had to leave. In the case of minority groups speaking a different language (Poles and Hungarians), Article 80 gave them the right to leave the state in six months and live in a state of their choice. Married women were ordered to follow their husbands, and children under 18 to go with their parents. This covered the case of Hungarians living in southern Slovakia and Poles in the area of Tešín (Teschen) in Silesia (bordering Poland) who also resented Czech dominance and felt that their district should have been part of Poland under the right of self-determination.[13]

All could therefore claim Czechoslovak citizenship if they had been born within the frontiers of Czechoslovakia or had lived there during the war and still lived there. This allowed anyone with a reasonable claim to be a Czechoslovak citizen to apply. Many kept their Austrian identity while reluctantly accepting this.[14] Austrians or Germans who had founded a factory in what had become Czechoslovakia faced a simple choice: sell the company or take Czechoslovak citizenship. The majority swallowed their pride and opted for the latter.

It is doubtful whether the Czechoslovak government was wise to demand that a majority of board members should be Czechoslovak citizens. Taking this did not change the attitude of Austrians, Germans or Poles. Austrians, as Sudeten Germans insisted on being called, remained suspicious of Czechs and of the Czech government, believing that the government always favoured Czechs to the detriment of other nationalities.[15] This is clear from the example of Eric Pasold, born at Freissen in western Czechoslovakia into the Austrian textile firm, Erich Pasold & Sohn, who regarded himself first as Bohemian and later Austrian.[16] He came to England in the late 1930s, took British citizenship and founded the successful Ladybird textile company at Langley, but in his autobiography published forty years later in 1977, he was still critical of the 'Czech Mafia' and claimed that Czechoslovakia should never have been created, though he was full of praise for the Czech industrialist Tomáš Bat'a.[17] Tomáš Masaryk for his part hoped that in time Czechoslovakia would become a multi-cultural and multi-ethnic state like Switzerland, in which the different racial groups would live in harmony. If that had happened, the 'nostrification' policy would have been a valuable contribution to creating a common sense of Czechoslovak nationality.

Any hope of integrating the different national groups was shattered first by the Depression, which hit the Austrians harder than the Czechs and by the growing appeal of Hitler from 1933. For example, it was not until 1936 that the Moravia company at Mariánské Údolí near Olomouc carried out a survey of the workers and staff to establish the number of Sudeten Germans and Czechs.[18] Poles similarly harboured grudges against Czechoslovakia and were encouraged to demand the Tešín area in 1938 after Munich. The national identity of the directors had no effect on the success or failure of a firm and it was easy to get round the 'nostrification' law, as the following brief case studies will show. There is no means of knowing whether the government believed that this law would be effective, but it created some strange situations during the First Republic. As will be seen, the greatest obstacle to prosperity was the economic nationalism of the new Central and East European states, which sharply reduced trade between them as each tried to achieve economic independence.[19]

Oderberge Chemische Werke, a German company[20]

A good example of a company which was never really Czechoslovak is this chemical company in Bohumin in northern Moravia. Founded in 1902 by a German Jewish entrepreneur, Rudolf Goldschmidt from Breslau (now the Polish city of Wrocaw), the company was originally established to make aniline dyes for sale throughout the Habsburg Empire. Goldschmidt & Sohn were wholesale dye merchants and Rudolf established the Oesterreichischer Chemikalienwerke Rudolf Goldschmidt, with the help of the main aniline dye manufacturer, Farbwerke in Höchst am Main.[21] But in 1917 Goldschmidt decided that it would be better to make saccharine, partly because aniline dyes were not needed in bulk in wartime and partly because the severe sugar shortage had created a demand for a cheap substitute.[22] The decision to manufacture saccharine was economically and politically astute. In addition, sugar had formed a major export during peacetime and saccharine production allowed the government to divert more sugar to the export market.[23] The decision also enabled Goldschmidt to enter the important Habsburg market in cooperation with the major manufacturer of the product.

Goldschmidt established a larger company, the Oderberge Chemische Werke, with the principal saccharine manufacturer, Saccharin A.G.[24] The new firm moved its headquarters to Vienna, where the Union Bank provided facilities for issuing the new shares, valued at 4 million krone. The directors were German and Austrian businessmen, including the vice president of the Bund Oesterreichischer Industrielle in Vienna, a representative of the Oesterreichische chemische und metallurgische Produktion and members of the Union Bank, Saccharin A.G. and Rudolf Goldschmidt.

When the First Republic was created, most of these people were no longer eligible to form the majority of the board members because they were not Czechoslovak. Instead, Goldschmidt's close associate Georg Lövy, was appointed managing director and applied for Czechoslovak citizenship.[25] Later he was replaced as managing director by Dr Wondreys from the

Verein für chemische und metallurgische Produktion in Karlovy Vary, and Lövy became Goldschmidt's representative in Berlin. The board became Czechoslovak by gaining representatives of the Iivnostenská bank, Georg Lövy, representatives of former Austrian, now Czechoslovak, chemical companies in Ústi nad Labem and a number of Oderberge directors who took Czechoslovak citizenship. The shares were transferred from the Viennese Union Bank to the Czechoslovak Iivnostenská bank and business was transacted through the Mährische Agrarische und Industrie Bank in Brno and other local banks.

Real power was exercised, as before, by the partnership of Goldschmidt and Saccharin A.G., but now with the Iivnostenská bank in place of the Union Bank. The greater part of the profits – up to 40 per cent – went to Saccharin A.G. and the rest was shared between Goldschmidt and the Czech bank. The reason for these profits were the very high Czechoslovak price and the foreign sales to the world market through a German cartel. Oderberger did not attempt to sell large quantities in the former Habsburg lands. There were two reasons for these large payments to Saccharin A.G. The first was that when Oderberge had been established in 1917, it had to make royalty payments on saccharine production from its pre-tax profits. Saccharin A.G. was a major shareholder and also shared the final profit with Goldschmidt and the bank. However, this was not the only reason for the very high payments made to Saccharin A.G. After the Oderberge Chemische Werke had been established, it had applied to the Viennese cartel office for an official saccharine cartel price. It appears to have been the only company making this and had a state monopoly. Consequently, the price was high. After the creation of the First Republic, the company applied to the cartel office in Prague for an official Czechoslovak price. The Prague office, operating under the same rules as in Vienna, approved the price. What makes this decision important is that the price was again very high and saccharine formed the foundation of the Oderberge Chemische Werke's profits throughout the First Republic. Once established, this cartel price was renewed from time to time but did not have to be revised until April 1937, when the company applied for higher prices. It then became clear how high they really were. In a breakdown of manufacturing costs (in German) the Czech word *slunze* appears as a part of the price of raw materials: 34.64 kè of a total manufacturing cost of 42.43 kè, presumably per kilo.[26] This word does not appear in dictionaries, although it has been used as a general term for compensation.[27] Since there is no reference to the royalty payments to Saccharin A.G., *slunze* must refer to this. If it excluded the cost of overheads, the price of the raw material (coal tar, a by-product of coke making) was only 7.79 kè. The royalty payment was high because it was based on maximum sweetness. Much of the saccharine that was produced was in tablet form at a much lower level.

Although the Oderberge Chemische Werke had a majority of Czechoslovak directors on its board and appeared to obey the nostrification law, real power lay in Germany with Rudolf Goldschmidt and the directors of the German saccharine company. This was reinforced by the company's membership of the international saccharine cartel that was dominated by large German firms. Gradually, Oderberge Chemische Werke diversified into a wide range of basic chemicals, pharmaceuticals, and horticultural, agricultural and photographic products. Some were manufactured under licence from German firms, others were developed with the help of the Plausens Forschungsinstitut in Hamburg, or were developed jointly with other Czechoslovak (formerly Austrian) chemical companies. This never altered the fact that the basis of the firm's profits was always saccharine. Oderberge Chemische Werke was from its beginning dominated by German interests, worked closely with former Austrian companies and directed much of its commercial activities towards the German-speaking world. It made a profit throughout the First Republic by exploiting the Czechoslovak market and through cartel sales and was only nominally Czechoslovak.

Optimit: a Viennese Jewish company[28]

Optimit was founded in Vienna in 1863 by a group of Jewish business people: factory owners, textile merchants and their wives and business associates.[29] The main feature of this company is the way that the directors were able to draw on a wide variety of contacts in the Viennese Jewish community for capital, ideas and entrepreneurial expertise. This was crucial to the development of the new products, which are a feature of this company.

Optimit was originally named after the founders, Schneck & Kohnberger, whose first venture was to buy a textile mill and spinning works at Odry and Benešov in northern Moravia. They survived the industrial depression of the late nineteenth century by producing high quality goods that were exhibited at the Viennese World Exhibition in 1873. By the beginning of the nineteenth century, they had developed a new line of business, making industrial drive belts. To be able to move from textiles to rubber technology shows not only an unusual scientific knowledge but also an awareness of new industrial trends.[30] The old system of driving machines from overhead shafts with long leather belts was being replaced by electric motors and rubber belts.[31] Within a short time the company had established a good reputation for these belts, made from bonding strong textile thread into rubber.

The creation of the First Czechoslovak Republic forced the group to choose between losing the factories or dividing the business. They chose the latter, for it was difficult for those established as manufacturers and merchants in Vienna to leave their firms. The company was divided into two parts: Schneck & Kohnberger remained as a trading organisation in Vienna, the Czechoslovak manufacturing side became Optimit gumové a textilné závody a.s.[32] A public announcement in the *Prager Tageblatt* on 12 December 1922 announced that Optimit had taken over the 60-year-old company Schneck & Kohnberger. New shares were issued to a value of 11 million kè and underwritten by the Allgemeine Böhmische Bank in Prague. The requirements of the nostrification law were met by creating a board consisting of four men who lived in Czechoslovakia: a Czech lawyer, Alois Brunèlik, a company employee, Viktor Irmenbach, and two representatives of the Allgemeine Böhmische Bank (both Jewish general managers of the bank) and Conrad Tiring and Carl Mislap, who had Viennese addresses.

In reality, there was no change in ownership from the old company Schneck & Kohnberger to the new Optimit, apart from changing the bank. At the head was the managing director, Conrad Tiring, born in Turkey in 1861, who had married Irene Kohnberger, daughter of one of the founders of the company. He and Carl Mislap owned a majority of the shares and held 611 of the 1,100 votes. Other major figures in the company were Johanna Mislap, Jakob and Melanie Herrmann, Frau Schüller, Carl and Martha Pollack, Dr Sigmund Stiassney and his daughter Liesbeth and Alfred Popper. All were members of the Viennese Jewish business community. They mostly lived in the Innere Stadt in Vienna and represented the respectable, prosperous Jewish middle class.[33] This remained the pattern of share ownership throughout the period to October 1939. When the company issued more shares, many were bought by Conrad Tiring, who felt a sense of responsibility for the firm through his marriage. Others passed from shareholders to their relatives and friends, but they always kept control within the Jewish Viennese commercial group that had created the company.

One of the important results of this continuing link between Odry and Vienna was that the company continued to do much of its trade with Vienna. This placed Optimit in a very good position, because Austria was the only Central European state that did not try to limit trade. Indeed, Austria made great efforts to continue trading with her former commercial partners, though without much success.[34]

Although control of the company did not change, the directors were aware of the need to bring in outside technical and scientific talent when necessary. In 1926 two scientific experts, Dr Weil and Dr Tichy, were appointed to the board.[35] The following year a Prague industrialist, Dr Emil Kepka, was appointed and later, in 1936 after the Depression, five more, including a factory owner, Hugo Rainer. None of these six men appears to have been Jewish. Although the owners wanted to keep control in their own hands, they recognised the need to recruit the most able men for the work.

There are three important features of this firm. The first is the way that the directors invested in new equipment and maintained the efficiency of their factories. The second is the work of the research and development team who changed from cotton to woollen textiles and looked for new ideas for using rubber technology. The company records contain many patents in Czech, English, German and French, which covered developments in America as well as in Europe. Out of this work came the production of inflatable rubber boats that continued during the Second World War, a design for a self-sealing motor tyre and a range of fine rubber thread for elastic. This led to the third feature: the drive to expand by setting up branches in England, Germany and America.[36] The success of this policy is evident from the financial records, which except for small losses in the early 1930s, show a profit in every year. This wholly Jewish-owned company kept its links with Vienna from the time it officially became Czechoslovak to its seizure by the Germans in October 1938. It proved a great advantage since Austrian trade was profitable and tariffs lower than those of other states. The nostrification law had been obeyed, but the owners' loyalties lay elsewhere.

Brankauer Draht-Blechwaren und Nägelfabrik; from Czechoslovak to American control[37]

Founded in 1863 by a Czech, Carl Dobrazil in Hradec nad Moravici in northern Moravia, the company produced locks, machinery, nails, shoe tacks, sheet metal ware and castings in the nineteenth century. The directors were a cross-section of the local community: Czechs, Austrians and Poles. Before the creation of the Czechoslovak state the board consisted of a number of local dignatories: the chairman Eduard Nedela, was a local councillor; Heinrich Janotta was President of the Opava branch of the Silesian chamber of industry and commerce, Franz Hammer was a factory owner and councillor, and Rudolf Pollak a director of the local branch of the Viennese Union Bank. The only changes in 1919, when the First Republic had been created, was that these men had lost their Imperial titles and the company changed its bank. As a group they matched the ideal of a new Czechoslovak company, owned and run by a mixture of Czechs and Germans. However, in less than ten years it was being run by Americans, apparently at a loss. Why it continued to function as a company and how this change occurred is the subject of this section.

For the first three years of the Czechoslovak Republic, the company had a market from Warsaw to Rome and as far east as Lemburg (Lvóv).[38] Brankauer was profitable: 1.01 million kè in 1919, 2.8 million kè in 1920 and 0.8 million kè in 1921. In 1919, in addition to home sales of 14.5 million kè, Brankauer had exported goods via Vienna (5.6 million kè), Poland

(2.6 million kè), Italy (2.3 million kè), Yugoslavia (1.8 million kè) and Bulgaria and Romania (200,000 kè each). There were also sales in the Middle East in Constantinople, Cairo and Alexandria. After 1921, the situation rapidly deteriorated. Currencies in the successor states to the Habsburg Empire declined in value and the countries raised tariff barriers as they tried to develop their own industries.[39] To try and achieve this they erected tariff barriers to hinder imports. The combination of currency instability, war (in the case of Poland), revolution (Hungary), tariffs and the high value of the Czechoslovak crown made it very difficult to achieve the same level of sales. What was worse, many of Brankauer's products were relatively unsophisticated and while they had been suitable for Central and Eastern Europe, they could not easily be sold in Western Europe or in the world markets. In addition, there was catastrophic inflation in Austria and the lock and sheet metal cartel, the Schlösserwaren und Blechwaren Verband was destroyed. Brankauer turned to Linke-Hoffmann A.G. in Breslau for machinery to improve the quality of its pressed metal products but could not afford to join the German Blechwaren Verband, which demanded caution money of 50,000 kè.[40]

In 1923, when the post-war boom collapsed, the board pinned their hopes on a building boom, expecting that many houses would be built for an anticipated influx of Czechs to counterbalance the large number of Poles in the area.[41] If this had happened, Brankauer would have been well placed to supply metal window frames, door and furniture locks, castings for ovens and stoves. Brankauer supplied these to the well-known hardware company Moravia, as well as a great many house building materials that would have guaranteed the company's prosperity.[42] The building boom failed to materialise, however, and the new tariff barriers damaged exports.

In this crisis, the board decided to turn to a German lock making company for help. This proved to be the first step in the loss of control. Brankauer's main products were locks and Damm und Ladwig not only produced their own but were also linked to the great American giant Yale and Towne. For Brankauer, facing bankruptcy, this appeared to offer access to modern locks that could be sold profitably at home and abroad. The price for this cooperation, and for a loan, was that Damm und Ladwig would be given two seats on Brankauer's board, 800 shares and Brankauer would pay a 7 per cent royalty on all Damm und Ladwig locks. The new German directors were Damm, managing director of the German company, and a lawyer, Dr Richard Frowein.

This failed to halt the decline; Brankauer's losses continued. The reason was that the Eastern markets did not need the more sophisticated – and expensive – German locks in sufficient quantities. There were cheaper alternatives available from Hungary and, protected by the high tariffs, simple locks and other equipment could be made locally. In 1927, in an attempt to improve the situation, Damm und Ladwig provided Brankauer with new lock designs and cheaper raw materials. Foundry production was improved and management changes were planned. But Brankauer still made losses.

The company's shares had declined in value and many shareholders sold their shares. Only two men owned at least 1,000: Dr Friedrich von Koch of Berlin (previously of Bärenwald near Opava) and a Czech director, Dr Mitschka. Most of the remaining shareholders had 100 shares or less. The board decided that if Brankaer was to survive it had to raise more money. In January 1927 the board cut the value of each 800 kè share to 80 kè and issued 9,000 new shares with a face value of 400 kè, 3,000 of which were bought by Damm and Frowein. This brought the share capital to an official value of 6.9 million kè. As a result of the reorganisation of shares and the voting rights attached to them, Damm und Ladwig had 422 votes out of a total of 896. This marked the end of Brankauer's independence. What Brankauer may not have realised was that Damm und Ladwig were in turn controlled by Yale and Towne. Damm later said that he thought that Brankauer should have been closed at this point. It was still not profitable and to the Germans the prospects appeared bleak. They were overridden by the Yale and Towne board.

Yale and Towne took a much more optimistic view of Brankauer, but failed to appreciate the difficulty of trying to sell goods in Central and Eastern Europe. From the American point of view, it was an established company with a good record until 1923. The Americans knew that the factory was well equipped, it had a well-educated and trained work force and that if the quality of management could be improved it would be profitable. In addition, the Brankauer network of agencies would be useful for selling Yale and Towne's locks and door closers, but the Americans did not realise the need to expand sales through agencies outside Europe, as other Czechoslovak companies did. Yale and Towne's decision to expand their production and sales in Europe in 1927 – they created a new firm, Dulv A.G. at Velbert in Düsseldorf – made Brankauer an asset rather than a liability as far as the European market was concerned. The Americans transferred their Damm und Ladwig shares to Dulv, which disguised their control over it. Brankauer provided 1.8 million kè for the new company from the sale of their own shares and this integrated the Czechoslovak firm into Yale and Towne.

From 1927 to the German occupation in 1938 Brankauer was still nominally Czechoslovak, though in reality it was run by the Americans. According to the nostrification law it had to contain a majority of Czechoslovak directors, but real power was in the hands of the Americans. Yale and Towne's first step was to use American methods of management. In 1929, the Yale and Towne system of management reporting was introduced, which provided a great deal of statistical information on current sales and compared these with the previous year's performance. There was also a report comparing Brankauer with the new German company, Dulv. Yale and Towne decided in 1930 to appoint Allen, their managing director, to the Brankauer board to check on progress. Allen was able to see how Brankauer was coping with the Depression and he decided that the Czechoslovak company needed additional money to provide financial support during the crisis. A fund was established of $512,500 to be administered by three Czechs, the managing director Juraèek and two directors, Rossmanith and Flohr. This stopped Brankauer going bankrupt. The trading position in 1930 was very bad: total sales had fallen by one-fifth and there were debts of 3.2 million kè. Total orders had declined and home sales had fallen more than exports. The company was still owed 150,044 kè from 1929 and exports to most countries had halved. Yale and Towne reacted by reducing the workforce by 35 per cent (from 534 to 348) and the office staff from 60 to 44. When this failed to solve the problem, the wages were cut each year until 1933 and the range of goods was also reduced.

When the market began to improve in 1934, Yale and Towne signed an agreement with Brankauer for the latter to make the full range of Yale products. On the surface, this was a contract between equals. Yale provided full plans and supervised production, the goods were stamped with the Yale trademark and were sold to customers chosen by Yale and Towne. The reality was that Yale dictated the terms: there was no closing date for the contract and no provision for ending it.

At this point it would have been better if Brankauer had been bought by the Americans and openly integrated into the American network of factories in America, Canada, Britain and Germany. If that had been done it would not have had to pay royalties on producing Yale goods, interest on the loan would have been transformed into investment and the Americans could have introduced any form of management without levying charges. But that was impossible under the nostrification law. Instead, Brankauer had to pay 11 per cent interest on all loans, royalties on production and $250,000 a year for management and production advice. As a result, the accounts showed a loss every year. It is not clear whether the money due to Yale and Towne was all paid or whether it was noted in the accounts as a debt. One result was that it made relations within the company much worse, as the directors found it impossible to free the company from this burden of debt and make a profit. This helped to cause a major row between the German director, Damm, and one of the Czechs, Krebs. Both were forceful and experienced characters and under normal circumstances would have been an asset to the firm. Pressure of continued losses finally created a crisis and Damm resigned. One of the results was that the German works manager, Mundt, lost a valuable ally. When Czech-German relations worsened in the later-1930s, Mundt found it more difficult to work efficiently and he was dismissed.

By 1935 the Americans had done all they could to improve Brankauer's prospects, but losses were continuing. As a last resort they sent an American, Kadisch, to be vice president and general manager. He proved a good choice. He came to the problems without any preconceived ides and as German-Czech relations worsened, he was neutral. He was able to make savings by substituting Czech steel for Swedish and local foundry sand for expensive German sand. A Swiss expert, Fluck-Meyer of Buttikon-Schweiz, was hired to advise on improvements to the foundry. Kadisch also discovered that an important agent, Wunsch and Vogel, with branches in Austria and Czecho-slovakia, was selling goods made by another firm and pretending that they were Yale and Towne products. This was a sign of the popularity of Yale goods. On taking legal advice, Kadisch found that it would take too long to bring the matter to court and instead collected the money owed and can-celled the agency. In so far as Brankauer could be made profitable under these conditions, Kadisch was successful, a view supported by another Yale and Towne director, Rolph, who was also monitoring his progress. By the time the Germans occupied the factory in October 1938, it was a successful firm. During the German occupation, freed of the financial burden of interest payments, royalty and management charges, it was profitable. Without the restrictions of the nostrification law, it would not have had to carry the heavy financial burden and would probably have been profitable earlier.

Conclusion

These three case studies of different types of Czechoslovak companies show that the nostrification law, though understandable in terms of Czech fear of Austrian influence on the fledgling state in the early 1920s, was unnecessary. It was also a contributory factor to the growing autarky that was a feature of the economic policy of all the successor states in the inter war period. The nostrification law had no effect on the way that these three companies were run, nor on their pattern of sales. Where it proved a dis-advantage was in the case of Brankauer, where it would have been better if the company had been openly owned by Yale and Towne and fully inte-grated into the world market. That would have given better sales and higher profits.[43] Instead, the company had a succession of losses, which proved an additional stress on the board and contributed to a major boardroom row between two directors, Czech and German. These three brief case studies also show differences in management styles between the American stress on business efficiency and the German and Czechoslovak use of cartels. It is likely that the Czechoslovaks, like the Germans, used cartels to improve the technical excellence of their products. It was essential that all members of the cartel produced goods to the same standard and cartel meetings provided an opportunity to share information. But the Oderberger Chemische Werke had the advantage of close links with the major saccharine producer and did not need any further help. But other companies normally joined cartels when trade became difficult and no doubt benefited from this.[44]

The example of Brankauer also shows the difficulty that the Americans experienced in understanding the depth of national feeling in the Successor states formed from the Habsburg Empire and which did so much to limit opportunities for trade in Eastern and Central Europe between the wars.

The government wanted companies to be profitable so that they could generate tax revenue and provide employment. The profits of all three companies depended on the ability of the directors to meet the demands of the market at home and abroad. In each case, the board of directors was more concerned with profitability than with cultural differences between Czechs, Germans and Austrians until the rise of the Sudeten German party in the mid 1930s. In the long run, the nostrification law proved unnecessary, since although it satisfied Czech pride, it could easily be evaded and brought no positive advantages.

Notes

* I am grateful to the British Academy for helping to fund the research of which this forms part.

1 The German-speaking people living in the area now known as the Sudetenland called themselves Austrians until the rise of the Sudeten German party. Then they began to call themselves Sudeten Germans to link their political party with Hitler's Germany.

2 J. W. Bruegel, *Czechoslovakia before Munich; the German minority problem and British appeasement policy* (University Press, 1973), p. 14. The Austrian Social Democrats were the largest Austrian party; they made their offers on 10 and 12 October; Frederick Hertz, *The Economic Problem of the Danubian states; a study in economic nationalism* (Gollancz, 1947), p. 64.

3 For the Czech case, see Josef Chmelaø, *The German problem in Czechoslovakia* (Orbis, 1936), passim.

4 For the Austrian case, see 'Diplomaticus', *The Czechs and their Minorities* (Thornton Butterworth, 1938), passim.

5 F. P. Habel, *The Sudeten Question* (The Sudeten German Council, 1984), p. 5.

6 According to the first census, in 1921, there were 6.7 million Czechs, 3.1 million Germans (former Austrian citizens), 2 million Slovaks, 0.7 million Hungarians, 0.5 million Ruthenes, 0.3 million Jews, 0.1 million Poles, Habel, *Sudeten Question*, p. 6.

7 Národní Vbor – National Committee.

8 Fred Hahn, 'The German Social Democratic Party of Czechoslovakia 1918–1926' in J. Morison (ed.), *The Czech and Slovak Experience* (Macmillan, 1995), pp. 203–17.

9 Zdenek Kárník, *Èeské zeme v éøe První republiky (1918–1939); díl první, Vznik, budování a zlatá léta republiky (1918–1929)*, [*The Czech state in the period of*

the First Republic, the rise, creation and golden age of the republic 1918–1929]
(Nakladatelství Libri, 2000), p. 41.

10 A. Teichova, 'Industry' in M. C. Kaser and F. A. Radice (eds), *The Economic History of Eastern Europe 1919–1975* (Clarendon Press, 1985), p. 295.

11 A copy of the relevant articles is in the regional archives in Opava, records of the Reichs Präsident, papers on German citizenship, È. kart. (inventory number) 1782. After the German occupation of the Sudeten area in 1938, the German authorities clearly had to remind themselves of the articles of the treaty that had established citizenship in the Czechoslovak state.

12 This did not solve the question of nationality, but only of citizenship. Austrians still referred to themselves as Austrians (though they held Czechoslovak passports). Two men who went to Leicester to manage a branch of the rubber and textile company, Optimit a.s., described themselves as Austrians, though they had previously lived and worked for the company in Odry in Czechoslovakia; regional archives in Opava, records of the Leicester branch of Optimit, Inv.È. 140.

13 This is why the Czech authorities tried to deny Slonzaks (Polish Slnzaks) the right to Czechoslovak citizenship. Under the terms of the Treaty they had to leave, though this would not stop them working in Czechoslovakia if they lived just across the frontier.
    Slonzaks were Galician Poles who did not share the same Polish culture as other Poles (many were Lutherans and not Catholics and spoke a different dialect). The Czech authorities wanted to raise the ratio of Czechs to Poles in the Tešín area to justify keeping it in Czechoslovakia.

14 One example is Hans Ledwinka, who became the chief engineer for the Tatra motor company. He was born at Klosterneuburg near Vienna but spent most of his working life at the Tatra factory in Kopøivnická, J. Sloniger, 'Hans Ledwinka' in R. Barker and H. Harding, *Automobile Design; Great Designers and their Work* (David and Charles, 1970), pp. 115–6. It led to many charges of collaboration after the war and was used to help justify the expulsion of the majority of the Sudetens in 1945 and 1946. Those considered pro-Czech were allowed to stay and re-wrote their names in a Czech style.

15 The Czechs claimed that because more business was in Austrian hands than Czech, the government was justified in discriminating in favour of Czechs. The Czech government denied that this happened, Eric Pasold, *Ladybird, ladybird, a story of private enterprise* (Manchester University Press, 1977), pp. 120, 165–6.

16 *Ibid.*, p. 38.

17 *Ibid.*, pp. 31, 166, 204.

18 But not for the last time. The German occupying authorities repeated this in 1940 to show that the great majority were German; Olomouc regional archives, records of the Moravia company, Details of company census, Inv.È. 28.

19 Hertz, *Economic Problem of the Danubian States*, pp. 53–91.

20 The records of this company are in the regional archives in Opava.

21 Farbwerke was originally Lucius and Brüning.

22 Most sugar was either bought by the army for making into glycerine for explosives or sold to neutrals; the civilian population had special sugar ration cards. A. Rasin, *Financial Policy of Czechoslovakia during the First Year of its History* (Clarendon Press, 1923), pp. 150–1.

23 Later, in the early 1920s, sugar formed almost 20 per cent of Czechoslovak exports; Z. Drabek, 'Foreign trade performance and policy' in Kaser and Radice (eds), *Economic history of Eastern Europe 1919–1975*, p. 403.

24 Formerly Fahlberg List.

25 He was subsequently referred to at times as Jiøi Loevy to make him appear Czech.

26 kè = Èesky korune = Czechoslovak crowns.

27 It has been used for compensation given to soldiers who had to pay for accommodation when they were away from their barracks. I am grateful to Ing. Kraus for this information.

28 The records of this company are in the regional archives at Opava.

29 This section is based on the company records in the Opava regional archives unless otherwise stated.

30 In the opinion of Meldau, a German patent lawyer, in 1943 the drive belts were of a high quality; Inv.È. 109, 7 June 1943.

31 Although electric power was being developed – 750 power stations had been built in Germany by 1900 – it was used mainly for trams and lighting. The big German electrical companies had already been formed. Georg Siemens, *History of the House of Siemens, vol. 1, the Era of Free Enterprise* (Freiburg/Munich: Karl Alber, 1957), p. 152.

32 Optimit rubber and textile company.

33 Their share certificates give their Viennese addresses, Inv.È. 9.

34 Austrian average tariffs were lower in 1927 than in 1913; all others were higher; Hertz, *Economic problem of Danubian States*, p. 72.

35 The board had a maximum membership of 14; Protokoll, 14 Dec. 1922, Inv.È. 9.

36 The self-sealing tyre was based on 1931 Czech patents and was tested by the Germans in 1943, using a variety of forms of artificial rubber [*buna*]. They tended to overheat and deform; Prüfung Bericht, Semperit Gummiwerke A.G., Traiskirchen, 1 Dec. 1943, Inv.È. 140. The English branch of Optimit was at Leicester, the centre of the elastic industry and the Optimit representatives, Mislap and Popper, are recorded as Austrian, not Czechoslovak. The firm was seized as enemy property in 1939; the American branch did not last long after its foundation in 1931, the German branch tried to take over the patent rights and name of the company in 1940.

37 The records of this company, Branecké železárny a.s. [Brankauer iron works] are in the regional archives in Opava.

38 This was the company's traditional market; Opava regional archives, records of Brankauer, liquidation balance, 28 Feb. 1919, Inv.È. 137. Unless otherwise stated, references to this company are to the company records in Opava.

39 General tariff levels in the Central and East European states in 1927 ranged from 30 per cent (Hungary) to 67.5 per cent (Bulgaria). Austria, which tried to encourage trade, had a general tariff of 17.5 per cent. Hertz, *Economic Problem of the Danubian States*, p. 72.

40 Brankauer, Verwaltungsrat minutes, 20 Nov, 1923, Inv.È. 13.

41 When the Czechoslovak—Polish frontier was agreed, this area was disputed. Many Poles lived in the area and expected that under the principle of self-determination it would become part of Poland. The Czechs, however, were determined that it would form part of Czechoslovakia because it contained coal mines that supplied the Vitkovice iron and steel works and the main railway line linking Czech to Slovak lands south of the Carpathians. The area south of the Olša river was occupied by armed Czech police and many Czechs were brought to live in the area.

42 Moravia's factory was at Mariánské Údolí, close to Ololouc. It was an important manufacturer of stoves, ovens and kitchen ranges for domestic and commercial use and bought castings from Brankauer.

43 Details are in the Brankauer archives, Profit and Loss accounts in Inv.È. 13.

44　During the inter war period most companies joined cartels as a matter of course. One exception was Tatra a.s., which made cars, lorries and other vehicles. There was only one attempt to create a cartel of vehicle manufacturers in 1930 but it quickly collapsed. It is unlikely that Tomáš Bat'a joined a cartel of shoe manufacturers. The history of his company, continued by his son, was of a constant drive to dominate the Czechoslovak market and move into world production; Anthony Cekota, *Entrepreneur extraordinary; the biography of Tomas Bata* (Rome: Edizioni Internazionali Sociali, 1968) [father] and Thomas J. Bata, *Bata; shoemaker to the world* (Stoddart, 1990), [son], passim.

3 The making of a puzzling industry

Historical perspectives on Japan's petrochemical industry

Meng Li

Introduction

The rise and fall of the major industries in post-war Japan was predetermined by government policies. At the same time, the government dominance of the directions of establishment and growth of each industry has first been praised and then criticized by scholars and industries.[1] Still, the conclusions about this dominance are mixed in many respects, and the government – industry relationship created by the Japanese has both its followers and detractors in the world. The history of Japan's chemical industry is a classic case. It became a rising star in the 1950s during the post-war period and was regarded as most attractive in the 1960s. Since the mid-1970s, however, the industry has been treated as one of the 'troubled industries' by the Ministry of International Trade and Industry (hereafter, MITI). This phenomenon has been labelled the 'Japanese puzzle' or 'paradox'.[2]

The Japanese petrochemical industry was naturally a substantial part of this puzzle.[3] The emergence and evolution of Japan's petrochemical industry demonstrated the first endeavour of latecomers in science-based industries after the Second World War.[4] The industry underwent a dramatic growth in the first fifteen years from almost scratch and continued staggering in the recession afterwards, trends that preoccupied many economists and management scholars. At the same time, few of them looked at the early period of the industry in retrospect to seek an understanding of the underlying institutional and technological establishment that has long been influencing the whole spectrum of industrial evolution.

It is not easy to unearth from historical clues systematic evidence of the causes of the puzzle. First, the development stage of the industry in Japan occurred in a harsh milieu of international complexity in which political factors were far more intricate than the economic. Secondly, the developing pattern of the industry was significantly different from the traditions developed in pioneering countries such as Britain, Germany and America, which made existing analytical tools less effective. The strategies of individual firms strictly adhered to the general national strategy associated with *keiretsu* (business groups) interests, by which corporate strategy and its influence on a firm's future performance limited the development of the necessary research base.

Initial conditions are crucial for the longstanding success of a petrochemical industry, not only because of the huge sunk-cost investment of the industry, but also because of the creation of the industrial structure shaped by the primary attitudes of all actors. The long-term success of the industry strongly links with economies of scale and scope that depend on a healthy industrial structure and the ease of accessibility to natural resources.[5] However, natural endowments, capital and a specialized knowledge of chemistry and chemical engineering were scarce commodities in Japan at that time.

This study re-examines the early stage of the industry from the early 1950s – represented by the emergence of 'nurturance' policies for downstream synthetic fibre and synthetic resin industries at MITI – to the eve of the first oil shock in 1973 – represented by the impending industrial troubles. It is possible to observe the causality between the formation of industrial structure and 'tender-hand' intervention, as well as accommodations in strategic government investment by a combination of policy instruments. All of these factors contributed to the industry's competitiveness in a specific environment, the intimate elements of the socio-economic underpinnings, and the logic behind the decision-making by each party. The study also explores the idiosyncratic effect of *keiretsu* groupings and the complementary role of industry associations in linking government organizations and firms to accommodate the interests of *keiretsu* groupings and government goals by means of formal and informal forces.

Challenging reality in the 1950s

The wars of the 1930s and 1940s, combined with the petroleum boom and progress in polymer technology, changed the overall course of Japan's energy structure and chemical industry. During the Second World War, Japan was isolated by the United States from access to any technological advances, while the oil supply had been cut off in 1941. Coal-based chemistry and fermentation-based technology were the only options for Japan, while in other parts of world, especially in the United States, it was a 'golden age' when petroleum-based chemical technology made enormous gains. Petrochemical technology combined polymer chemistry with chemical engineering technology, on which most basic research, initial pilot trials and technology development, industrial

R&D, and knowledge diffusion, as well as investment in plant, was led by enormous American, German and British companies in the pre-war and inter-war periods. In the Western world, this technological advance, symbolized by new, economical synthetic processes, new product lines, and pervasive commercialization of polymers, was booming.[6] Because the information flow to Japan of technological advances in the field during the pre-war period was slow, and almost disappeared completely during the war, once Japan decided to utilize petroleum-based knowledge it was not surprising that petrochemical technology would almost wholly rely on foreign technologies for a substantial period.[7] As Table 3.1 demonstrates, an enormous gap in both polymer science and chemical engineering existed between Japan and the leading countries.

The Korean War (1950–1953) provided the opportunity for Japan's rapid economic recovery, as well as providing access to technological information about petrochemicals. The relationship with the United States changed, given that a resumption of war between two countries was no longer an issue.[8] To some extent, the Korean War aggravated the uncertainty in coal imports from Korea and China, but global petroleum oversupply in the 1950s created a trend toward the use of this cheap form of energy. These energy, capital and technology concerns prompted Japan to make the strategic decision swiftly

Table 3.1 The Gap in Major Polymers between Japan and Leading Countries

Polymer	World[a]	Japan	Lag in years	Leading Country
Vinyl Acetate Monomer (VAM)	1924	1936	12	Germany
Polyvinyl Chloride (PVC)	1929	1933[b]	4	US
Styrene Monomer (SM)	1930	1959	29	Germany
Polystyrene (PS)	1930	1957	27	Germany
Low-density Polyethylene (LDPE)	1933	1958	25	UK
Styrene Butadiene Rubber (SBR)	1937	1960	23	Germany
Polyamide (PA) (Nylon)	1938	1950[c]	12	US
Polyurethane (PU)	1940	1954	14	Germany
Ethylene	1942	1958	16	UK
Silicone (SI)	1943	1956	13	US
Acrylonitrile-butadiene-styrene (ABS)	1947	1963	16	US
Epoxy Resin	1947	1961	14	Switzerland
Polyethylene Terephthalate (PET)	1949	1957	8	UK
Polyoxymethylene (POM)	1956	1968	12	US
High-density Polyethylene (HDPE)	1955	1958	3	Germany
Polypropylene (PP)	1957	1962	5	Italy
Ethylene Vinylacetate Copolymer (EVA)	1963	1967	4	US

Notes: a For the first commercialization in the world.
b Nippon Zeon got a PVC technology licence in 1952.
c Toyo Rayon (now Toray) got the Nylon Licence from DuPont in 1950.

to switch the coal-based chemical industry to petroleum. When a number of oil refineries along the Pacific coast were allowed to reopen in 1949 and overseas petroleum capital flooded in, a transition became possible, albeit one dependent on foreign technology and capital (see Table 3.2).[9] This transition had a far-reaching influence on the subsequent investment policy in the petrochemical industry.

Moreover, the dramatic transitions characterized by an energy structure shift, post-war economic reconfigurations and technological progress, heightened the socio-economic tensions between existing coal-based chemical companies and rising oil refineries, local interest groups and foreign capital, *keiretsu* groups and non-*keiretsu* enterprises, firms and labour unions, and indigenous research and technology importation. These tensions called for the government to arbitrate in reconciling conflicts and play a leadership role in devising tariff protection for the incubating industry, as well as taking precautions against cut-throat competition in the industry.[10] Thus, government intervention was considered a necessary measure for late-developing countries to catch up to their more developed rivals.

Although the boom fuelled by war demand was interrupted by the armistice in 1951, and the consequent ending of the war in 1953 stopped the rapid inflow of hard currency, the surge of imported chemicals persisted.[11] Previous studies of the incubation period of development were often preoccupied with the importance of the special military procurement by the US forces during the war and considered thus to provide the initial capital accumulation that laid the foundations of ensuing growth.[12] Indeed, the government took considerable advantage of this at the time, including considerable financial and technological assistance from the US government. This was aimed at deterring the spread of communism in Asia and to help the post-war economic recoveries of its allies in the region, and to mobilize all the national resources toward economic autonomy after regaining state sovereignty in the early 1950s.[13]

At the same time, the government's bigger plan beyond dealing with immediate goals was to return to the international economic community,

Table 3.2 Foreign Capital Invested in Japan Oil Refineries

	Japan Partner	*Ratio %*	*Year*
Standard-Vacuum Oil Co.	Tonen Fuel	55	1949
California Texas Corp.	Nippon Oil Refinery	50	1951
Caltex Oil Products Co.	Toa Petroleum	50	1950
Tide Water Associated Oil Co.	Mitsubishi Oil	50	1940
Anglo-Saxon Petroleum Co.	Showa	50	1952

Source: JPCA, *Ten-Year History of Petrochemical Industry*, p. 37.

represented by membership of the International Monetary Fund (hereafter, IMF), the General Agreement on Tariffs and Trade (GATT), and the Organisation for Economic Co-operation and Development (OECD), all of which called for a transition towards an open economy.[14] Calling for economic autonomy, combined with easing the potential pressure of import and export payment imbalance, required the government to take urgent measures to revitalize the economy by promoting exports and securing domestic production before the liberalization of trade and capital investment. Under the umbrella of a national strategy, MITI felt it had a reasonable legitimacy to guide Japan's industries by a well-organized industrial policy.

A key industry selected

After industrial rationalization, priority production and signing the San Francisco Peace Treaty, an ambitious government formulated a growth plan.[15] Since it had so many experiences with world powers in its development, MITI did not find it difficult to pinpoint its ultimate target: technologically sophisticated manufacturing industries such as automobiles and electronics. But before that could be achieved, the material bases to support these strategic industries had to be firmly secured. As a consequence, the heavy and chemical industries emerged as key industries in the 1950s.[16]

Primary measures were taken to select the strategic basic material industries such as steel, chemicals and cement, which were regarded at that time as the secure upstream sectors for downstream industries, including narrow-focused exporting industries such as textiles, shipbuilding and machinery. The petrochemical industry was given the highest priority on MITI's nurturance list.[17] The essential rationale for this priority was the industries' unique weight in basic materials and the great potential of the sophisticated technologies embedded in its processes. Petrochemical technology was not only directly linked with important imports like petrochemicals and exports like textiles, but it also provided the enormous technological base for other industries and other aspects of society. This base included a variety of new products, new processes, new raw materials and new end markets. A comment from a JPCA publication revealed the essential judgment at that moment:

> . . . at the centre of policy for a self-supporting economy are the encouragement of export and improvement of self-sufficiency rate, for which it is necessary to push forward aggressively. On the other side, the necessity of the policy for the export encouragement must be emphasized based on a sophistication of Japan's industrial structure as a whole. The modernization of facilities in the existing basic industries

such as electricity, coal, steel, and shipbuilding has been realized, and now it is necessary to nurture emergent industries, such as synthetic fibres, synthetic resins, petrochemicals, and electronics.[18]

The other justification for the administrative role of government in microeconomic intervention was that only government could 'actively foster' a favourable environment and amass all the advantageous forces of the nation for exporting products. Some industries, including the petrochemical industry, obviously were assigned roles as supporting actors. The government owned unique resources, including financial instruments, redistribution of wartime state-owned assets and mobilizing ability, and it possessed supreme authority in approving any new large-scale investment.[19]

Barriers to entry in capital, technology, information and learning and management – as a market mechanism of the heterogeneity of potential entrants and their future development – were overcome by approvals, pricing control, rapid and collective intra-industry technology spillovers, and information diffusions. The approval mechanism determined the sequence of market entry, but had difficulty doing so without commitment of opportunity equity for the losers in the previous entry competition, considering the tradition of reciprocal consent among potential actors in one industry and the complexity of post-war political situations in the nation.[20] The purpose of sequential entry was to prevent the infant industry from excessive competition in both investment and market and keep a 'healthy industry order'. Thus, selective government intervention in economic development faced few obstacles and often was praised by the industries. Based on a consensus of industry groups, the government decided to help firms rapidly overcome a lack of three factors in productivity: technology capability, chemical knowledge accumulation in individuals, and the limited domestic demand for petrochemicals.

Two more factors were often unnoticed in the prior studies about the industry. The union unrests in the 1950s and the 1960s were little documented and ignored.[21] Even though unionization was not an urgent factor for the petrochemical industry, it was significant enough that MITI had to consider its agenda as a whole.[22] A MITI official expressed the agency's thinking as follows:

> . . . without such industries (including petrochemical industry) it would be have been extremely difficult to employ a population of 100 million and raise their standard of living . . . Logical or not, Japan had to have their heavy and chemical industries.[23]

Other factors to be considered were the electoral and regional. Increasing chemical incidents and pollution in the areas of petrochemical complexes

Table 3.3 Tax Incentive and Tariff Relief for Petrochemical Projects (in billion yen)

	Technology Import				Research Expenditure			
	Total	Subtotal	Tax Reduction	Tariff Reduction	Subtotal	Machinery	Trial	Tech
1956	3.1	3.1	0.6	2.5	–	–	–	–
1958	6.1	4.5	1.0	3.5	1.6	1.6	–	–
1960	8.9	7.4	1.4	6.0	1.5	1.5	–	–
1962	12.0	9.5	0.5	9.0	2.5	2.5	–	–
1964	16.8	9.8	0.8	9.0	7.0	6.3	–	0.7
1966	10.6	6.7	0.8	5.9	3.9	–	1.3	2.6
1968	15.3	–	–	–	15.3	–	11.0	4.3
1970	19.1	–	–	–	19.1	–	13.0	6.1
1973	24.3	–	–	–	24.3	–	19.8	4.5

Source: A. Goto, 'Gijyotsu seisaku [Technological policy]', in R. Komiya, M. Okuno, and K. Suzumura (ed.), *Nihon no Sangyo Seisaku [Japan's Industrial Policy]* (Tokyo: Tokyo University Press, 1984)

became political issues in elections that made politicians exert pressure on location planning.[24] These factors meant the government had to balance the powers of each interest group when it planned to implement its general strategy.

The development of the petrochemical industry paralleled the structural shift from inorganic to organic orientation within the chemical industry, as well as obviating the production vacuum in petrochemicals and high polymer materials.[25] The oil-refining industries expressed their intent to enter the new industry. So did the existing chemical industries, such as producers of carbide, soda, fermentation, and fertilizers, because they saw the cheerful prospect of entering the petrochemical industry and the dim prospect of continuing with their existing old technologies and production modes. The government's target scheme and variety of incentives were other attractions of the new industry (shown in Table 3.3).

Competing for 'land'

One of the important components of the Japanese management system is pre-emption of land ownership. Having land is the necessary condition for entry into the petrochemical industry. The development of the industry began with the expected competition for the ownership of the former military fuel facilities through intense debates and enduring interactive processes. The role of the government and activities of industry groups and firms in the course of privatization are described in appendix 2.

For speeding up the development and concentration of the scarce capital, austere governmental controls on market entry, coupled with the significant incentives of subsidiaries, drove players to exercise lobbying powers via internal workings of institutions from the beginning of the industry. The result of all of this was that the owners of the facilities or land would become the first entrant groups in the industry and enjoy substantial government support.[26] Government criteria strictly stipulated that only groups were eligible for the procurement of former military fuel-asset sites (see appendix 2). The result as anticipated was that the members or their alliances from three ex-*zaibatsu* (Mitsubishi, Mitsui and Sumitomo) were granted ownership of the three sites. A new location (the Kawasaki complex near Tokyo) from the old sites was granted to the important group of non-*keiretsu* players as a balance-of-interest distribution in the then star industry.[27]

Industry dynamics

The early development of the industry was divided into three phases, each with a definite goal:

> Phase One (1955–1959): Complete prevention of polymer importation.
> Phase Two (1960–1964): Technology upgrade and cost reduction.
> Phase Three (1965–1972): Establishment of world-class plants.

In Phase One, the central theme was to produce synthetic resins locally, instead of importing them. Another central theme was mastery of key petrochemical technologies. The four companies with good financial background and chemical experience led the early entry as the core member of each complex. The core members possessed the ethylene centres. Mitsubishi Petrochemical Corporation (hereafter, Mitsubishi Petrochem), Sumitomo Chemical Company (Sumitomo Chem), Mitsui Chemicals Inc. (Mitsui Chem) and Nippon Petrochemical Company (Nippon Petrochem) were selected to be the first companies to enter this new industry around 1955.[28] The 'import-stemming effect' was introduced to quantitatively monitor technology importation efficiency, which is the relationship between technology and goods exported.[29]

MITI hoped the first entrants would undertake an experimental course and accumulate experience for the later entrants. With regard to technology screenings and approvals, one case is interesting: each company chose a different polyethylene technology and foreign licensor (see Table 3.4). Sumitomo Chem chose ICI's LDPE technology, because it was familiar with ICI's process and assumed that quick licensing from ICI would accelerate its leading position in LDPE production.[30] It became the first LDPE producer in 1958, one year ahead of Mitsubishi Petrochem, which used BASF's LDPE technology. In Mitsui Petrochem, the technology selection underwent a hot

Table 3.4 Technology Selection for Polyethylene in Phase One

Manufacturer	Technology Supplier	Capacity, by (Year)
Mitsubishi Petrochem	BASF	10,000 (1959)
Sumitomo Chem	ICI	11,000 (1958)
Mitsui Petrochem	Hoechst (Ziegler)	12,000 (1958)
Kokawa Chem	Standard Oil of Indiana	9,000 (1959)
Nippon Olefin Chem	Phillips	10,000 (1959)

Source: adapted from JPCA, *Ten-Year History of Petrochemical Industry*

debate over Ziegler's unique patent on HDPE technology filed in 1953. This technology was licensed in 1955 to Mitsui Petrochem, because it supposed that Ziegler's process was cost-effective based on its experience with synthetic oil. It is difficult to understand from historical records whether these selections were purposeful or not; but for the nation as a whole, the multiplicity of technology did provide excellent opportunities for technology learning and spill-overs within the petrochemical and chemical industries.

The commitment to late entrants was obvious as the whole journey was prearranged, considering the entry approval and increasing propensity to egalitarianism in Japan. The first bloc was just short of a head start and any pre-emption on individual expansion or entry was prohibited. Three years later, in Phase Two, five new entrants as new core companies in ethylene centres were ratified to join the petrochemical club, at that time the most attractive industry in terms of either industrial growth or governmental support and protection. As the first bloc's average capacities were small and the newly constructed capacity was much larger, to compensate the first bloc MITI and the industry association called attention to the stable operation of the first bloc. The four existing companies were consequently given precedence over new entrants in expanding their production capacities (shown in Table 3.5).

The first bloc's total net increase in capacity was comparatively higher than the total capacity of the new entrants. It is remarkable that Mitsubishi Petrochem was the lowest in the net capacity increase in the first bloc. However, in order to compensate Mitsubishi Chem, a second independent player from the Mitsubishi group was allowed to start up in the industry. Another apparent trend was how upstream petroleum and mining companies descended into the downstream ethylene and derivatives industry and giant steel and textile enterprises started engaging in the petrochemical business.[31] The configuration of the industry became more complicated as numerous makers from different industries participated (demonstrated in Figure 3.1). However, the target of cost reduction to a level of the average international price was never realized.

Table 3.5 Ethylene Capacity Expansions during the Three Phases (thousand ton)

	Phase 1 (1955–59) Increase Capacity	Phase 2 (1960–64) Increase		Phase 3 (1967–72) Increase		Average Capacity By Bloc
		Net	Capacity	Net	Capacity	
Nippon Petrochem	25	75	100	100	200	
Mitsubishi Petrochem	22	60	82	600	682	
Mitsui Petrochem	20	120	140	120	260	
Sumitomo Chem	12	74	86	460	546	
Subtotal	79	329	408	1280	1688	422
Tonen Petrochem			63	422	485	
Maruzen Petrochem			44	400	444	
Daikyowa Petrochem			41	300	341	
Mitsubishi Chem			45	115	160	
Idemitsu Petrochem			100	200	300	
Subtotal			293	1437	1730	346
Showa Petrochem					150	
Osaka Petrochem					300	
Mizushima Ethylene					300	
Sanyo Ethylene					300	
Subtotal					1050	263
Aggregated total	79		701		4468	

The third phase was kicked off in 1965 when Japan surpassed Germany to become the second largest chemical economy. There was little difference between the procedures of this third phase and those of the previous phases: new entrants into the ethylene project had to follow the new capacity criteria; old entrants were awarded capacity expansion ahead of new entrants, even though total ethylene capacity was excessive for the country. Many factors also confined the plants capable of economies-of-scale in polymeric materials such as polyvinyl chloride, polystyrene and polyethylene to one location. Institutional arrangements restrained effective expansion by means of vertical and horizontal integration within and across groups. Before the first oil shock of 1973, a structural issue had emerged, although the entry approval system continued. In addition, government as both planner and judge on entry could not escape commitment for the entire arrangement and was in an inflexible position on any readjustment.

Growing tensions

Scholars of post-war Japanese industrial development have given far more attention to the reciprocal consensus in Japan than to the conflicts and tensions

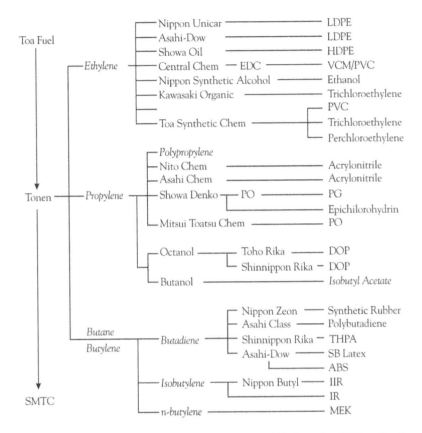

Figure 3.1 Producer and Product Alignment in Kawasaki's Petrochemial Complex 2

Source: Nihon Kagaku Kai [Japan Chemistry Society], *Nihon no Kagaku Hyakunenshi* [*Century History of Japan Chemistry*] (Tokyo: Tokyo Kagaku Dojin, 1978), p. 816.

between the Japanese government and industries in prior studies. As widely perceived, in the early development phase government was concerned with industrial structures and orders, as well as with the overall performance of industries. However, firms care more about their own competitive status and probability of survival in the market. In the long run, the government's high priority was to improve employment, prepare for liberalization of the economy, and increase the standard of living. It wanted to seize the 'divine-wind' to quickly eradicate backwardness, to reach its dream of being a strong nation in all ways.[32] In the short term, its unambiguous goal, except for political performance within each incumbency, was to foster targeted industries, promote public good, and improve the import-export balance.[33]

MITI's strong preference for the joint operation by groups in individual petrochemical complexes made it difficult to achieve both horizontal integration and subsequent economies of scale. In addition, sequential entry made it impossible for early entrants to use any effective strategic entry-deterring practices to preclude the risk of excess capacity.[34] Fundamentally, given the policy of equal opportunity on entry, this impeded the formation of big businesses. Under this process, any pre-emptive action to initiate and expand production scale was prohibited not because of antitrust concerns, but to maintain equality and balance the power of *keiretsu* groups and regions.[35] This approach, which was somewhat harmless in industries such as textiles, machinery, and even automobiles, prevented the companies with the potential for growth from obtaining the returns on scale investment that are vital to the international competitiveness of an industry like petrochemicals. This policy design prevented the growth of the competent companies, but retained small producers. In addition, government policy, as reflected in the Petroleum Industry Law that protected the upstream petroleum industry, impacted negatively on the petrochemical companies. The naphtha issue amplified the conflicts resulting from this policy arrangement.[36]

Keiretsu and the organizational capabilities of individual firms

There has been a debate among scholars on decision-making in the industry. The essence of the discussion is how each firm built up its capability under the shadow of *keiretsu* configuration and the interplay among *keiretsu* members. One argument regarded *keiretsu* groups as decision-making bodies; another saw member enterprises as primary actors. The former recognized the dominance of *keiretsu* groups in a full range of industrial activities that weakened the individual function of member firms in decision-making processes. The latter insisted that the momentum for enterprise growth should be within the enterprises themselves and that *keiretsu* groups should just play a complementary role. The cases of Mitsubishi Petrochem and Mitsui Chem appeared to justify the former argument, but other cases and the long-run evolution of the industry justified the latter.[37] However, in contrast with Western experience, one fact was obvious, that the collective actions of *keiretsu* member firms showed a propensity towards intra-group business tie-ins.[38]

Petrochemical firm as manufacturing plant

The historical fact was that few individual Japanese firms at the very beginning could meet the requirements of finance and technology for investment in such a capital-intensive, technologically-complex industry. To make earlier entry possible and maintain industrial dynamics, the only option for each firm was appealing to group backup for channelling in government loans, tax incentives, and specialists, which was consistent with MITI's strategy.[39] Therefore, in the early phase the dependent status of member firms and constrained conditions in creating organizational capabilities were unsurprising. The collective effort to import different technologies and rapidly diffuse learning prevented duplicative endeavour and increased group profits, but management responsibility did not transfer to the leading companies. *Keiretsu* member firms did enjoy the benefits of sharing technical knowledge, technology diffusion, and management knowledge. More importantly, in the high-growth period, cosy business relationships within group networking enabled each firm to speed up the pace of technology assimilation and to organize learning in narrow sub-fields. Stable business ties within groups and import protection policies provided a good growth climate for early entrants. Figure 3.2 represents the typical supplier affiliation under *keiretsu* control.

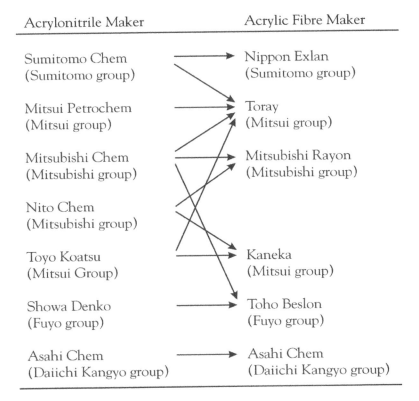

Figure 3.2 Supply Relationship of Petrochemicals for Textiles

Besides the supply pattern, to some extent sales rights went to trading companies of each *keiretsu* group. In this early configuration, individual companies in the industry actually served as manufacturing plants for an entire *keiretsu* group. Internal efforts within *keiretsu* groups shaped group behaviours of a generation of top managers in project execution and problem-solving in the process of technology transfer.

In return for the initial assistance, petrochemical firms had to make trade-offs with other members in the interests of sharing technology. *Keiretsu* groupings restricted the integration of companies across groupings; within the same *keiretsu* any potential merger for expansion needed reciprocal consensus among related parties. A total of fifteen petrochemical complexes were dispersed in twelve regions. The dispersion made it difficult for potential leading companies to be integrated into more concentrated complexes capable of achieving economies of scale. The lack of economies of scale became a burden for Japan's petrochemical industry.[40]

By the early 1970s, industry overcapacity became an urgent issue after the three phases of dramatic development. Although overcapacity was a global phenomenon at the time, the differences in handling this diverged significantly.[41] Western countries undertook severe restructuring to revitalize their competitiveness. Considering the *keiretsu*'s characteristics, it was difficult for Japan's firms to use dramatic restructuring to overcome their difficulties.[42]

Grade differentiations as product strategy

One pervasive product strategy used by Japanese petrochemical firms was grade differentiations.[43] Tilton used the term 'technological hook' to describe the interdependence between petrochemical manufacturers and downstream users.[44] To cater to the needs of powerful industry customers, upstream companies made great efforts to customize commodities into specialties, thereby greatly increasing product grades.[45] As resource and capital scarcity made the country more sensitive to a reliable supply, downstream users developed a penchant for paying a premium to domestic suppliers in a favourable economic environment. These 'technological hooks' succeeded in creating barriers to entry for outsiders, but the sheer level of customization made the average cost of petrochemicals fifteen per cent higher than that of overseas competitors. It also made cost reduction complicated.[46] The reason for this is that it was imperative to hold domestic markets and meet group demands; it was a dangerous move to reduce cost by reducing customization of commodity products. The resulting reality was that these petrochemical manufacturers lost their global competitiveness that was based on cost advantage.

The proliferation of product grades also revealed the lack of professionals with a profound knowledge in chemistry and chemical engineering.[47] The

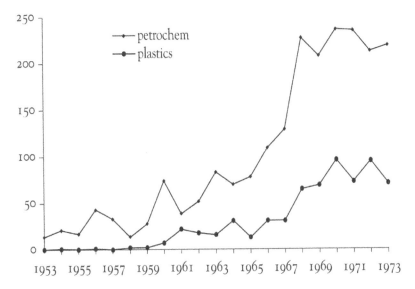

Figure 3.3 Imported Polymer Technologies, 1953–73
Source: Technology Import Report.

continual importation of technology was another reason for the shortage (as shown in Figure 3.3).[48] Massive technology imports shortened the technology lag in existing technology accumulation, but it did little to promote the mastering of inventive and innovative processes that is imperative for further development in any field. To a certain extent, technology importation limited the behaviour associated with seeking individual basic research and consequently influenced the establishment of substantial research competency and institutions.[49]

Incomplete organizational capabilities

Chandler argued that organizational capabilities are the main reason a company performs better than its competitors.[50] He defined the organizational capabilities as 'the collective physical facilities and learned human skills as they were organized within an enterprise'.[51] Chandler emphasized that these capabilities are achieved through the sharpening of time-consuming routines and building the institutions that enable a company to face market challenges and technology uncertainties. It is the first firms that make the three-pronged investments in production, distribution and management essential to exploit fully the economies of scale and scope that quickly dominate their industries.

In this sense, during its early development, Japan's petrochemical industry and companies focused on technology assimilation and diffusion, as well as on enlargement of physical capital. All these efforts were just part of their accumulating organizational capabilities. The development of other critical organizational capabilities, such as independent R&D, financial institutions, and marketing skills, was either ignored or deemed unimportant at the time. The attributes of Japan's successful industries – for example, incremental improvement in process by skilled and experienced workers, innovation through sharing tacit knowledge, increased product variety and complexity with focus on market niche, work flexibility and intimate supplier relationship – failed to exert an active influence in this industry.

Lieberman's insight into the chemical industry can explain the weak points in Japan's petrochemical industry in the perspective associated with information diffusion.[52] It is known that the major Japanese companies possessed similar strategies and broad-based chemical portfolios. His research pointed out that information diffusion often intensifies the competitive process and suggested that internally generated learning should be kept proprietary for an extended period of time to protect the company's investment and future competitiveness.

Industry association and *Kondankai*

The *Kondankai* (nominally, an informal communication group) in Japan could take an informal or formal form, but it was important for formulating government policy. The Petrochemical Technology *Kondankai* provided the basic outline for technology orientation and scale; the *Kondankai* on Basic Issues of the Chemical Industry addressed petrochemical industrial structure and future international competitiveness; the Petrochemical Coordination *Kondankai* aimed at solving problems across industries. The Petrochemical Industry *Kondankai* appeared in 1957 to represent the collective interests of the industry. It succeeded in persuading government to grant tax credits and tariff exemptions, to offer low-cost loans, and to establish foreign-exchange quotas.[53] The Petrochemical Industry *Kondankai* was replaced by JPCA in 1958 as a formal mechanism for intra-industry coordination and external consultation, playing a pivotal role in the early development of the petrochemical industry. JPCA acted as a linkage between MITI and members of JPCA.

Concluding remarks: rapid entry and lock-in

The centre of Japan's high-growth economy after the Korean War was the large, capital-intensive manufacturing enterprises. To realize the government's strategic trilogy (developing key industries, encouraging low-price and securing strategic materials, and promoting exports), petrochemical firms, under the administrative guidance of MITI and facilitated by industry associations and *keiretsu* groups, achieved tremendous progress in technology and dominance of the domestic market. The timely acquisition of available technology laid an extensive technological base and greatly upgraded the whole knowledge level; what is more, modified technologies stemming from this base had already been exported to other countries, and net values of the import and export of foreign technologies had already contributed to Japan's economic growth. Seizing opportunities in a timely way was more critical than production efficiency. However, government intervention during the development of the industry shaped the unexpected industrial structure that disabled the industrial leadership of petrochemical firms and affected their later international competitiveness in more dynamic competition. This happened because of:

1   The government policy of overprotecting early entrants by entry approval and offering a variety of incentives created an artificially prosperous situation in the industry that induced too much attention from intra- and inter-industries in the sequential phases. Overemphasis on equal-opportunity entry and scattered location of complexes made achieving economies of scale impossible. The scarcer professionals were dispersed to numerous manufacturing firms and this to a certain extent hampered the formation of economies of scope. As a matter of fact, the surges of duplicative investment and endeavours in the industry with diseconomies of scale and scope had already formed the 'capacity bubble' and enlarged the structural flaws before the first oil shock of 1973.

2   Government intervention hindered the formative conditions and regularities regarding the achievement of economies of scale that are extremely important for long-term success in this industry. The government's multiple role at the microeconomic level made it difficult to insist on sound economic principles. Compromise and commitment to upstream petroleum companies and entry by firms without any chemical experiences were simple examples of the government's lack of focus on economic concerns.

3   The *keiretsu*'s advantage was in its ability to mobilize groups to cooperate towards the same end and in organizing collective learning, as well as technology and information diffusion, based on long-term ties. Since management responsibility did not transfer to leading companies, internal confrontations and accommodations, as well as separate activities for optimal growth opportunity in different complexes, made it impossible to achieve full-scale capabilities.

4   Because individual petrochemical firms in the early stage were treated as manufacturing plants of *keiretsu* groups, and because most technologies

had to be imported, the organizational capabilities of these firms compared to those of leading pioneers were incomplete. The resulting arrangement discouraged research and marketing efforts. These shortcomings vitally hindered the creation of critical strategic and core capabilities. The growing pains of petrochemical companies were reflected in their growth potentials resulting from R&D capabilities and market constraints because of technology licensing.

5   The industry association (*kondankai*) played an active and complementary role across *keiretsu* groups and industries. On the other hand, it became a lobbying arena and a kind of industrial cartel during the recessions.

Early active government intervention also prevented the government from following the German way of developing dyestuffs and the American way of developing petrochemicals after the First World War, both of which ways fostered a national infrastructure of science and technology and also economic institutions.[54] Except for cultural traditions and institutional heritages, the three factors of capital-intensive investment, *keiretsu* effect, and reciprocal consensus, created a dichotomy of industrial structure (that is, reliable but cost-ineffective, large but uncompetitive, proliferative but less innovative industry) and path-dependently determined the evolving industrial configuration. In conclusion, one should also note that government intervention in this industry almost immediately became a model of industrial policy not only for other Japanese industries, but also for other developing countries. This industrial policy provided an alternative means for latecomers in their ambitious catch-up plans in sophisticated industries.

Acknowledgement

Part of this paper was presented at the 48th Annual Meeting of Business History Conference at the Hagley Museum and Library, Wilmington, Delaware. The author thanks Professor Richard Rosenbloom and David Hounshell for their valuable comments.

Appendix 1: The formation of petrochemical industry policy

In 1951, the organic section of chemicals bureau of MITI issued the report 'on petroleum-based synthetic organic chemical industry' to direct the necessity of government nurturance policy. At the core of the policy of economic autonomy was the promotion of exports and increasing indigenous production of materials. In 1953, the nurturance policies for the synthetic fibre

and cellulose acetate fibre industry were passed by MITI to clarify the consolidation of production systems and import prevention. As the upstream
industry of the synthetic fibres and resins sector, the petrochemical industry
was supported by a resolution on 'Promotion of Synthetic Organic Chemical Industry' passed in the parliament in May of 1954 and a sub-committee
on promotion of chemical industry was set up in the House of Representatives. In July, a 'Nurturance Policy for Petrochemical industry' was passed
by MITI. In August, the sub-committee held a hearing into the government's
nurturance policy for petrochemicals that became the 'Outline of Nurturing
the Petrochemical Industry' in September. Based on the outline, the nurturance guideline for the petrochemical industry was formulated by July of
1955.

Supporting policies from government included special reimbursement on
important equipment; approval of overseas technology imports; loans from
the national development bank; legal personal tax relief and tariff exemp-
tion on imported machinery, as well as the special provision of foreign currency (See Figure 3.4).

Note: this part is based on JPCA, *Petrochemical Yearbook 1961*; S.
Hasegawa, 'Sekiyu kagaku kogyo no ikusei [Nurturance of the petrochemical industry]', in MITI Industrial Policy History Committee (ed.) *Tsusho
Sangyo Seisakushi [History of International Trade and Industrial Policies]*,
vol. 6 (Tokyo: Tsusyo Sangyo Choshakai, 1990), pp. 486–548;

Appendix 2: The privatization of former military fuel assets

The cradle of Japan's petrochemical industry was the former military facilities located in three important coastal regions: Yokkaichi (between Osaka and
Nagoya), Iwakuni and Tokuyama (in western Japan). The great efforts made
to acquire the strategic sites by *keiretsu* groups and major companies to form
oil refining, chemical, mining and steel industries offered the classic example
of government intervention and accommodating each interest group.

The former military facilities were the oil refineries for fuel supply: they
were the second navy fuel plant in Yokkaichi; the third navy fuel plant in
Tokushima, and Iwakuni Army fuel plant in Iwakuni. The Yokkaichi site
was the biggest and most modern. After the Second World War, these military sites were under the direct control of the Occupation Forces. In October
1945, GHQ of Allied Occupation Forces informally agreed to the Japanese
government's attempt to restructure the facilities into civilian production
(that is, as Nippon Fertilizer in Yokkaichi, Mitsubishi Chem in Iwakuni, and
Nippon Nitrogen Fertilizer in Tokuyama). However, in October 1946, the

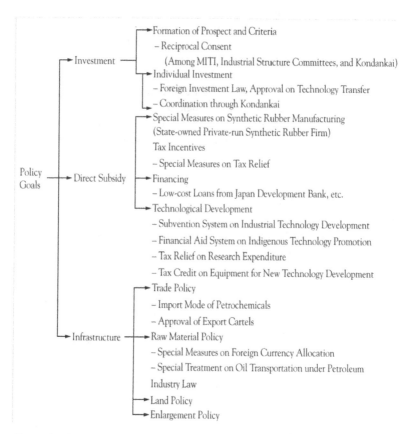

Figure 3.4 Policy and Instruments

Source: K. Yamamoto, 'Kagaku kogyo no setsubi ogataka to taisei seibi [Enlargement of facilities and restructuring in the chemical industry]', in MITI Industrial Policy History Committee (ed.), *Tsusho Sangyo Seisakushi* [*History of International Trade and Industrial Policies*], vol. 10 (Tokyo: Tsusyo Sangyo Choshakai, 1990), p. 336.

suspension of the scheme ended the preliminary round of tussles for these facilities.

The dramatic change of US policy to Japan in 1949 restarted the moves for these facilities. After the Peace Treaty was signed in 1952 that disclaimed Japan's war indemnity by US government, the bidding for the facilities became extraordinarily fierce. MITI designated ad hoc committee by the end of 1951 to formulate the guidelines for the privatization and debrief the proposals by participants and opinions of regional interests. The diverse proposals were distributed from individual procurement to collective operation or nationalization. By mid 1955, a new plan put forward by Minister Ishibashi of MITI was approved by Hatoyama Cabinet after long interactive discussions on the variety of proposals. The basic principle of the new plan stressed that one site had to be procured by one company, then the company had to cooperate with other companies for both petrochemical and oil refinery industries.

Yokkaichi navy fuel site

Eleven companies from petroleum, mining and chemical industries (Showa Petroleum, Tonen Fuel, Nippon Petroleum, Nippon Mining, Maruzen Petroleum, Daikyowa Petroleum, Koa Petroleum, Idemitsu Kosan, Imperial Petroleum, Mitsubishi Petroleum, and Tokai Ryoan) competed fiercely for the possession of this strategically important site. The first seven giants agreed on a proposal of Collective Operation on the site advised by five eminent figures of petroleum industry, but Mitsubishi Oil and Tokai Ryoan allied with Shell were absolutely opposed to the proposal. MITI put forward a state-owned private-run company called Yokkaichi Petroleum Company to force Mitsubishi to make compromise with the seven on the collective operation agreement in 1953, but the sudden failure of locating the Mutual Security Act Fund led to the success of the alternative petrochemical plan offered by Mitsubishi, Shell and Showa Petroleum in 1954. Showa Petroleum Company was allowed to procure facilities on the ground for oil refinery usage but the land was owned by the state; Mitsubishi Chem and Shell established a joint company annexed to Showa Petroleum's facilities in the way of petrochemical journey. Shell capital was not allowed to enter until 1957 as MITI insisted on its indigenization policy in the petrochemical industry.

Tokuyama navy fuel site

Idemitsu Kosan and Showa Petroleum tendered for the site for oil refinery usage. As Showa petroleum has been approved in Yokkaichi project, the ownership of the site was unsurprisingly assigned to Idemitsu Kosan who worked together with Sumitomo Chem in 1955.

Iwakuni navy fuel site

In addition, Nippon Petrochem composed of Asahi Chem, Asahi-Dow, Nippon Petroleum, Tonen Fuel, etc. in Kawasaki paid a different path out of observable influence of major keiretsu groups. Sumitomo did not directly join in the biddings for the sake of its own ammonia business. It was the only firm that enter the petrochemical field on its own Niihama site without involving other participants in the inception, but it got the government sub- vention for pilot trials of polyethylene and energy transition for ammonia production as well as technology cooperation with ICI.

After the settlement of the former facilities, the embryo of petrochemical complexes was formed by the interdependence of Koa Oil-Mitsui Petro- chem, Idemitsu Kosan-Sumitomo Chem and Showa Petroleum-Mitsubishi Petrochem directly or informally encouraged by MITI. Japan petrochemical industry began her unique voyage in exploiting new energy and as one of the key basic material industries.

Note: this is based on the following literature: JPCA, *Petrochemical Year- book 1961*; *Ten-Year History of Petrochemical Industry*; *Sekiyu Kagaku Kogyo Nijunnen no Ayumi [Twenty-Year Anniversary of Japan Petrochemi- cal Industry]* (Tokyo: JPCA, 1975); K. Yamamoto, 'Kagaku kogyo no set- subi ogataka to taisei seibi [Enlargement of facilities and restructuring in the chemical industry]', in MITI Industrial Policy History Committee (ed.), *Tsusho Sangyo Seisakushi [History of International Trade and Industrial Poli- cies]*, vol. 10 (Tokyo: Tsusyo Sangyo Choshakai, 1990), pp. 328–86; Mit- subishi Yuka Kabushiki Kaisha, *Thirty-Year History of Mitsubishi Chemical Company*; Sumitomo Kagaku Kogyo Kabushiki Kaisha [Sumitomo Chemi- cal Company Limited], *Sumitomo Kagaku Kogyo Kabushiki Kaisha Shashi [Corporate History of Sumitomo Chemical Company Limited]* (Osaka: Sumi- tomo Kagaku Kogyo Kabushiki Kaisha, 1981); Mitsui Sekiyu Kagaku Kogyo Kabushiki Kaisha [Mitsui Petrochemicals Inc.], *Twenty-Year History of Mit- sui Petrochemicals Inc.* (Tokyo: Mitsui Sekiyu Kagaku Kogyo, 1978);

Notes

1 C. Johnson, *MITI and the Japanese Miracle: the Growth of Industrial Policy, 1925–1975* (Stanford: Stanford University Press, 1982); E. Vogel, *Japan as Number One* (Cambridge: Harvard University Press, 1979); M. E. Porter and H. Takeuchi, *Can Japan Compete?* (London: Macmillan Press, 2000).
2 T. Hikino, H. Tsutomu et al., 'The Japanese puzzle: rapid catch-up and long struggle', in A. Arora, R. Landau and N. Rosenberg (ed.), *Chemicals and Long- term Economic Growth: Insights from the Chemical Industry* (New York: John Wiley & Sons, 1998), pp. 103–35; H. Itami & Associates, *Nihon no Kakaku Sangyo [Japan's Chemical Industry]* (Tokyo: NTT Shinbunsha, 1990).
3 The petrochemical industry mainly implies naphtha-derived products located in SIC 28. (Naphtha is the feedstock for producing ethylene and derivatives.) Petrochemicals accounted for 16.5% of the Japanese chemical industry in 1960; 31.1% in 1965; and 56% in 1970. See Japan Petrochemical Industry Association (hereafter JPCA), www. jpca. org. jp.
4 This movement in Japan became an example for other 'latecomer' countries.
5 A. D. Chandler, 'The enduring logic of industrial success', *Harvard Business Review*, 90(2) (March–April 1990), pp. 130–40.

6 The typical examples are a novel fixed-bed oxidation process in making ethylene glycol, Ziegler and Natta's organometallic catalyst system for making polypropylene, and Phillips' process for making crystalline polyethylene.

7 Japan recognized progress in petrochemical industry after they were allowed access to information from either the library of civil intelligence section of the General Headquarters (hereafter GHQ) or overseas tours permitted after the Second World War. See Sekiyu Kagaku Kogyo Kyokai [JPCA], *Sekiyu Kagaku Kogyo Sanjunnen no Ayumi [Thirty-Year History of Petrochemical Industry]* (Tokyo: JPCA, 1989), p. 3.

8 The main tasks of Occupation Forces were to dismantle the Zaibatsu war potentials, promoted emocracy and demand war reparations soon after the Second World War. The tasks were swiftly diverted to deter the spread of communism in Japan and other Asian countries after the burst of the Korean War.

9 Foreign capital accounted for major or equal stock share in the major oil refineries. The total foreign capital accounted for 25.4 per cent in Japanese oil refineries in 1958.

10 For the debates on the impact of massive technology transfer, see A. Goto, 'Gijyotsu donyo: sango nihon no keiken [Technology transfer: the experience of postwar Japan]', in Y. Kosai and J. Teranishi (eds), *Sango Nihon no Keizei Kaikaku: Shijo to Seifu [Economic Reform in Postwar Japan: Market and Government]* (Tokyo: Tokyo University Press, 1993); S. Kodama, *Kenkyo Kaibotsu e no Do [The Road to Research and Development]* (Tokyo: Tokyo Kagaku Dojin, 1978).

11 As a matter of fact, Japan had been heavily relying on imported coal and oil. The import prevention measures in the industry were to block the importation of chemical products rather than primary raw materials.

12 Special procurement contracts for the American military forces were worth $3.5 billion from1950 to 1955, which accounted for 44 per cent of total export revenue of Japan in that period. See K. Arakawa, *Nihon no Gijyotsu Saikou [Revisit Japan Technology]*, p. 16.

13 Porter and Takeuchi argued that western companies shared their knowledge freely and readily entered into partnerships that gave Japanese firms access to markets and technologies. Abegglen asserted that assistance for Japan was the US's grand plan to prevent communism spreading across Asia and Japan. See Porter and Takeuchi, *Can Japan Compete*; J. C. Abegglen, *The Japanese Factory: Aspects of its Social Organization* (Illinois: Free Press, 1958).

14 Japan joined the IMF and GATT in 1952 and 1955, respectively. Although the United States supported this move, European countries were against it, which held back Japan's full membership of GATT until (Article 11) 1963 and the IMF (Article 8) in 1964. Japan joined the OECD in 1964. In fact, the real liberalization of trade and capital in Japan did not begin until 1968.

15 R. Komiya, 'Josho [Introduction]', in R. Komiya, M. Okuno, and K. Suzumura (ed.), *Nihon no Sangyo Seisaku [Japan's Industrial Policy]* (Tokyo: Tokyo University Press, 1984), pp. 1–22.

16 In Japanese, Kikan Sangyo (Key Industry) is defined as the most important industry in a nation's economic activities that varied with different developing periods of economic growth.

17 JPCA, *Sekiyu Kagaku Kogyo Nenkan 1961 [Petrochemical Industry Yearbook 1961]* (Tokyo: JPCA, 1962), p. 52.

18 JPCA, *Sekiyu Kagaku Kogyo Junenshi [Ten-Year History of Petrochemical Industry]* (Tokyo: JPCA, 1964), p. 65. For the formation of petrochemical industry policy, see appendix 1.

19 During Meiji restoration and at wartimes, the similar approaches were frequently used, see D. E. Westney, *Imitation and Innovation: The Transfer of Western Organizational Patterns to Meiji Japan* (Cambridge: Harvard University Press, 1987); and R. J. Samuels, *Rich Nation, Strong Army: National Security and the Technological Transformation of Japan* (Ithaca: Cornell University Press, 1994).

20 The mechanism of technology approval in petrochemical industry did not end until in 1968 after completion of major technology importations.

21 The first waves of large-scale general strike for employment and labour rights reached the peak from 1950 to 1952. They were major in textiles, coal-mining, and chemical industries, but the impact was signal considering country's size, media coverage and political rivalry, see Nihon Kagaku Kogyo Kyokai [Japan Chemical Industry Association, JCIA], *Nihon no Kagaku Kogyo Sango Sanjunen no Ayumi* [*Thirty-Year History of Postwar Japan Chemical Industry*] (Tokyo: JCIA, 1975), p. 199.

22 It affected industrial rationalization policy and policy on small and middle enterprise, which forced government to make responding compromise and adjustments on the petrochemical project approval.

23 J. C. Abegglen and G. Stalk, Jr, *Kaisha: The Japanese Corporation* (New York: Basic Books, 1985), pp. 71–2.

24 In the 1960s and 1970s, the chemical incidents and pollution triggered thorny issues, see JPCA, *Petrochemical Industry Yearbook 1973*, p. 154.

25 From 1955 to 1960, inorganic chemicals declined by 19.4 per cent but organic ones including synthetic resins and organic synthetics raised by 23.4 per cent.

26 MITI stressed the effective utilizations of these old facilities from the beginning.

27 The group constituents were of importance. It was composed of rubber factories (Yokohama Rubber and Nippon Zeon), a joint venture (Asahi-Dow), traditional chemical firms (Asahi Chemical, Nippon Soda and Furukawa Chemical), steel maker (NKK), electrical manufacturer (Asahi Denko and Showa Denko) and gas and oil refineries (Tokyo Gas, Tonen Fuel, Showa Oil, and Nippon Oil Refinery).

28 Six Mitsubishi group members (Mitsubishi Chemical, Mitsubishi Rayon, Asahi Glass, Mitsubishi Bank, Mitsubishi Trading and Mitsubishi Metal/Mining), catered for government requirement on group approach and the need for symbiotic growth, established Mitsubishi Petrochem in 1956; Seven Mitsui group members including Mitsui Chemical, Miike Synthetics (later merged in the Mitsui), Toyo Koatsu, Toyo Rayon, Mitsui Mining, Mitsui Metal/Mining, and Mitsui Bank together with Toa Oil, formed Mitsui Petrochem.

29 The index equals the fraction of domestic demand for certain product by using imported technology and the sum of import amount and domestic demand for the product by the imported technology. If the product import becomes zero, the effect is 100 per cent and means completely domestic production of the product. Therefore, the 'import-stemming effect' is proportional to the reduction of import goods. The aggregate effect reached 70 per cent for chemicals in 1960; for synthetic resins and fibres, 100 per cent, see H. Arai, 'Gijyotsu donyo [The importation of technology]', in S. Nakayama (ed.), *Nihon no Kagaku Gijyotsu Toshi* [*The Social History of Science and Technology in Contemporary Japan*] (Tokyo: Gakuyou Shobo), p. 162.

30 Only Sumitomo Chem possessed some polymer knowledge. It was undertaking pilot trial of polyethylene with support from Kyoto University and research subsidies from MITI.

31 In the second bloc, Tonen, Daikyowa, Idemitsu, and Maruzen were oil refineries; in Phase One, they were naphtha suppliers of Mitsui Petrochem, Mitsubishi Petrochem, Sumitomo Chem and Maruzen group respectively. NKK, Nippon Steel, Toray, Teijin, Kurashiki Rayon (now Kuraray), Mitsubishi Rayon were involved in the industry during this period.

32 In *Rich Country, Strong Army*, Samuels gave pertinent analysis to this point.

33 Japanese government always is keen on preventing external payment problem. See R. P. Dore, *Take Japan Seriously* (Stanford: Stanford University Press, 1987), p. 197.

34 When a firm or group got the ownership of the former government-owned sites, one condition was joint operation of these sites with other firms. See JPCA, *Ten-Year History of Petrochemical Industry*, pp. 61–3.

35 A. Kudo, 'Sekiyu kagaku [Petrochemical]', in S. Yonekawa, K. Shimokawa, and H. Yamasaki (ed.), *Sango Nihon Keieishi [History of Postwar Japan Management]* (Tokyo: Toyo Keizai Shinbunsha, 1990).

36 As Japan is short of natural gas, naphtha takes over 95 per cent in total raw material consumption.

37 Sumitomo chemical from the very beginning worked as independent enterprise thanks to its own historical background. After about forty years, Mitsubishi Chem and Mitsui Chem finally merged Mitsubishi Petrochem and Mitsui Petrochem respectively in 1990s.

38 M. L. Gerlach, *Alliance Capitalism: the Social Organization of Japanese Business* (Berkeley: University of California Press, 1992).

39 Mitsubishi Chem tried to cooperate with foreign capital (Shell), but the government policy is to discourage the majority of foreign capitals in the industry. See Mitsubishi Yuka Kabushiki Kaisha [Mitsubishi Petrochemical Company Limited], *Mitsubishi Yuka Sanjunenshi [Thirty-Year History of Mitsubishi Petrochemical Company]* (Tokyo: Mitsubishi Yuka Kabushiki Kaisha, 1988).

40 The cost of raw materials was 1.6 times higher than Europe; 3.6 times US, see K. Watada,'Petition on Countermeasures against Trade Liberation in the Petrochemical Industry', in JPCA, *Petrochemical Industry Yearbook 1961*, p. 555.

41 Some authors suggested the overcapacity could be as the strategy approach to deter further entry. See M. B. Lieberman, 'The learning curve, technology barriers to entry, and competitive survival in the chemical processing industries', *Strategic Management Journal*, vol. 10 (1989): pp. 431–47. It is difficult to discern that the strategic move was leveraged or not but in fact the overcapacity did discourage local players' and foreign giants' entries into Japan's petrochemical industry.

42 As mentioned above, even within the same keiretsu group, it took over forty years for Mitsubishi Chem to merge Mitsubishi Petrochem.

43 P. Herbig, *Innovation Japanese Style: A Cultural and Historical Perspective* (Westport: Quorum Books, 1995); and see I. Nonaka, 'Product Development and Innovation', in K. Imai and R. Komiya (ed.), *Business Enterprise in Japan: Views of Japanese Economists* (Cambridge: MIT Press, 1994).

44 M. Tilton, *Restrained Trade: Cartel in Japan's Basic Materials Industries* (Ithaca: Cornell University Press, 1996).

45 Take polyolefin products as an example, Japan's product grades are 8.3 and 5 times more than those in US and Europe respectively; for polypropylene product, the grades are 20 and 12 times respectively.

46 Hikino *et al.*, 'The Japanese puzzle: rapid catch-up and long struggle', p. 110.
47 The higher education on chemistry and chemical engineering was initiated late in Japan. For specific reason, the talented students seemed to favour normal engineering and electronics and dislike chemical-related disciplines.
48 In terms of polymer technology, it is strongly linked with organic chemistry, catalyst technology, structural chemistry knowledge and development in polymeric chemistry and physics. In these disciplines, then Japan's strengths did not give prominence.
49 Arai, 'Gijyotsu donyo [The importation of technology]', pp. 167–8.
50 A. D. Chandler, 'The competitive performance of U.S. industrial enterprise since the Second World War', *Business History Review*, 68(1) (Spring 1994), pp. 1–72; A. D. Chandler, 'Organizational capabilities and the economic history of the industrial enterprise', *Journal of Economic Perspectives*, vol. 6 (Summer 1992): pp. 79–100.
51 A. D. Chandler, *Scale and Scope: The Dynamics of Industrial Capitalism* (Cambridge, Harvard University Press, 1990), p. 594.
52 M. B. Lieberman, 'The learning curve and pricing in the chemical processing industries', *Rand Journal of Economics*, 15(2) (Summer 1984), pp. 213–28; M. B. Lieberman, 'The learning curve, diffusion, and competitive Strategy', *Strategic Management Journal*, vol. 8 (1987), pp. 441–52.
53 JPCA, *Ten-Year History of Petrochemical Industry*, pp. 98.
54 J. P. Murmann, 'Knowledge and competitive advantage: the co-evolution of firms, technology, and national institutions in the synthetic dye industry, 1895–1914', *Enterprise and Society*, 1(4) (2000), pp. 699–704; J. P. Murmann and E. Homburg, 'Comparing evolutionary dynamics across different national settings: the case of the synthetic dye industry, 1895–1914', *Journal of Evolutionary Economics*, 11 (2001), pp. 177–205; D. C. Mowery and R. R. Nelson, *Sources of Industrial Leadership: Studies of Seven Industries* (New York: Cambridge University Press, 1998); H. G. Schroter, 'The German question, the unification of Europe, and the European market strategies of Germany's chemical and electrical industries, 1900–1992', *Business History Review*, 67 (Autumn 1993), pp. 367–405.

4 Corporate governance and public policy

'New' initiatives by 'Old' Labour
to reform stakeholder behaviour in
the UK, 1965–1969

Sue Bowden and Andrew Gamble

Introduction

Under-performance, be it in terms of absolute or relative productivity, exports, market share or profit growth, has bedevilled the UK economy for decades. There is now a voluminous literature charting evidence for under-performance.[1] Less well understood is why under-performance was allowed to continue. At the micro level of the firm, the long twentieth century has witnessed a switch in the ownership and management of the firm in the UK. The owner-managed firm has been replaced by the predominance of the limited liability company and a divorce of ownership from control. Management is in the hands of a professional managerial group, few of whom (until recently) hold equity in the company. Ownership is in the hands of thousands of individual and institutional shareholders, few of whom hold a sizeable percentage of the equity in any one company, none of whom have sufficient equity to influence management, but all of whom have an interest in the current and future earnings from their equity holdings.[2] Can we link this under-performance to these changes?

Two strands in the literature suggest important, but to date unrelated, factors. The first emphasises public policy regimes, most notably in terms of anti-competition policy and extensive government intervention in both the macro and micro level.[3] According to this view, under-performing firms were allowed to survive, sometimes with public monies, whilst regulation and intervention in the form of industrial, regional and employment policies made it difficult for managers to 'manage'. The emphasis here is on industrial policy with the target being individual firms and/or sectors and the emphasis on managers of industry. Taken to its logical conclusion, this view would suggest that policy acted to distort the operation of market forces, competition was constrained, and the exit process (which prompts the demise of the inefficient and acts as a spur to the more efficient) not allowed to function.

The second strand emphasises the role of the 'City'. Adherents of this view point to two issues. They would first class industry as the 'victim' of short-term strategies by investors from London-based financial institutions as firms were 'forced' to prioritise dividends at the expense of investment whilst being 'starved' of capital for investment.[4] Under-performance is linked to constraints on investment following from the pressure to prioritise dividends. Their second concern relates to the dilution of responsibility as the equity of publicly quoted companies is shared between thousands of individuals and institutions. The incentive for owners is to exercise the right to transfer property rights in shares, by off-loading shares in under-performing companies on the stock exchange. The attraction of this second 'City' view, from our perspective, is the stress on ownership responsibilities and the constraints on their fulfilment.

Firms, owners and managers all operate in a political environment. Prevailing public policy regimes influence their strategies and actions. It is now a truism that public policy regimes have and continue to influence the development and practice of corporate governance in the USA,[5] but the notion that this might apply in the UK appears to have been overlooked.[6] It is not inconceivable that institutional shareholders have been influenced by fear of greater government regulation of the financial institutions and by public ownership policies.[7] Both could act to deter shareholders from intervening in the case of under-performance, not least because the latter offers the promise of a transfer of ownership responsibilities from owners to government. The structure of share-ownership and the prevailing public policy regime could act together to persuade institutional shareholders to adopt arms-length relations with firms and to enhance any latent propensity to stress ownership rights rather than ownership responsibilities. Equally, government may influence behaviour via administrative and legalistic changes relating to company law in terms of the internal mechanisms of corporate control, not least in the conditions whereby directors are appointed, information made available (company reports) and financial information verified (the audit process).

The potential of public policy to affect the behaviour of both owners and managers is therefore great. How and why public policy regimes have interacted with and influenced the behaviour of both shareowners and managers is less well understood. Nor do we have any long-run perspective on how and why specific reforming attempts by 'modernising' governments have influenced the development of corporate governance in the UK. This paper addresses such issues by an examination of the interplay between public policy regimes and 'City'–industry relations in the first Wilson Government.

We assess the attempts made by that Government to influence both the internal and external mechanisms of corporate governance. The former stressed an administrative solution. We consider three specific initiatives: those of government as 'corrector' of the market mechanism, the attempts to reform company law and developments in notions of the 'stakeholder firm' in modern society, and the responsibilities of government as shareholder. The second area of policy concern, which ran in parallel to the administrative initiatives, involved active intervention to prompt take-overs. We assess the take-over initiatives in terms of Government/City relations and the long-run effects of Government intervention on the subsequent behaviour of institutional shareholders and hence the evolution of corporate governance in the UK. The initiatives taken together illustrate the development of ideas on best practice in corporate governance and show how, in many ways, the Wilson Government predicted many of the contemporary debates on the role of the firm in the modern economy and had, both in their initial proposals and ultimate failure, important long run implications for the development of corporate governance in the UK.

Public record office files from the Board of Trade, the Department of Economic Affairs, the Treasury, and the Ministry of Technology, together with the detailed records kept by and recently released by the Industrial Reorganisation Corporation provide the key qualitative primary source materials. They have been supplemented by our second key primary source materials, i.e. company share registers which have allowed us to identify the share holdings and transactions in specific company shares by named 'City' institutions, together with market price data and contemporary financial press comment and evaluation of stocks.

Section II assesses the policy options available to Government and identifies the key problem as that of reforming corporate governance without alienating the financial markets. Section III examines attempts to influence governance by the 'administrative solution'. Section IV reviews evidence on the behaviour of the financial institutions, whilst Section V details the implications of Government intervention in the financial markets via the 'take-over solution'. Section VI considers why the initiatives on stake holding and shareholding were aborted and the long run consequences for the development of corporate governance in the UK.

II

The Labour Government's (1964–1970) priority was to achieve 'greater economic growth'.[8] An essential part of the plan was 'to break out of this vicious circle (the periodic balance of payments crises which checked economic expansion) and to introduce and maintain policies which will enable us to enjoy more rapid and sustained economic growth'.[9] Rapid and sustained growth would result from the modernisation of the British economy. Industrial efficiency was the name of the day. This had six components: standardisation, rationalisation, management education, industrial investment, the efficient use of labour and an acceleration of technological advance throughout industry.[10]

The problem was how to realise these objectives. Two of the six components quickly became the focus of particular attention: the structure of industry and the quality of management. The two were highly inter-related. Government believed that long-term growth and prosperity depended on the international competitiveness of UK firms. Industry, it was believed, was not large by international standards; even larger firms were agglomerations of disparate activities.[11] As such, economies of scale could not be realised and research and development could not compete on an international scale. Change was called for.[12] The aim was not to eliminate competition but to create firms able to compete in global markets; competition was directed to global not national markets. Only large firms could benefit from new technology and, as such, prosper in the international economy: 'the need is for structural change to take advantage of technological developments'.[13]

Rationalisation was not deemed, by itself, to be sufficient. A second, but by no means secondary, objective was to improve the quality of management. Technology would only be effective if accompanied by 'modern' management capable of introducing, monitoring and implementing it. As the *National Plan* noted, 'the most intangible and yet by far the most important factor in improving industrial efficiency is the quality of management'.[14] The thinking was that industry needed a new brand of management, aggressive in its determination to win export markets and effective in its ability to deliver productivity growth. Both required openness to new technology and an ability to manage its implementation.

The aim, therefore, was to produce large, technologically advanced, modern firms run by 'modern' management, which would have the financial, marketing and research resources to manage technology and, as such, match those of the UK's main competitors.[15] To identify the structure of industry and the quality of its management as major constraints on technological innovation, and hence on international competitiveness, was one thing. To correct the constraints was another, not least since both raised questions as to the ownership of industry and the responsibilities of owners, and, in so doing, meant that the financial institutions as major shareholders of British industry would be affected and involved in any policy strategy the Government pursued. The Government's view was that markets had failed to deliver large, modern firms, run by efficient management, able to compete in the global market place: owners in these terms had failed to deliver. Government, if it were to realise its objective of rationalising industry and improving the quality of management, would have to persuade owners of the merits of its case.[16]

The first issue was the identity of owners. There were two dimensions to this. First, the twentieth century had witnessed a dilution of ownership; by the mid 1960s, ownership of publicly owned companies was spread amongst thousands of shareholders.[17] The second was the rise of the institutional investor (Table 4.1), who by the 1960s was accounting for the bulk of the new money coming into the London Stock Exchange. In 1963, institutional investors owned 26 per cent of the ordinary shares of listed companies; this had risen to 37 per cent in 1969 and 40 per cent by 1970.[18] Within the total, the proportion of shares held by the insurance companies grew to 12.2 per cent in 1969, pension funds to 9 per cent and unit trusts to nearly 3 per cent (Table 4.1).[19] Together, the dilution of ownership and the switch from private to institutional equity owners meant the Government would be dealing with City institutions as the main shareholders of publicly quoted companies.

The second issue was the lack of clarity over what responsibilities shareholders (and directors) had. Matters were not helped by legal vagueness as to the definition of ownership rights and responsibilities. The only legal right that the principal had (and still has) related to dividend income: the rights to the residual income of the company or the surplus accruing after all the company's contractual obligations have been met. What responsibilities are incurred was, and still is, less obvious. In theory, the owner (the principal) has the right to hire and fire management (and determine their

Table 4.1 Distribution of Shareholdings by Beneficial Owner

	Percentage of market value in issue		
	1963	*1969*	*1975*
Persons	54	47.4	37.5
Charities, etc.	2.1	2.1	2.3
Insurance companies	10	12.2	15.9
Pension funds	6.4	9	16.8
Unit trusts	1.3	2.9	4.1
Investment trusts, etc.	10	8.7	10
Stockbrokers and jobbers	1.4	1.4	0.4
Banks	1.3	1.7	0.7
Non-financial companies	5.1	5.4	3
Public sector	1.5	2.6	3.6
Overseas sector	7	6.6	5.6
TOTAL	100	100	100
Total market value (£ million)	24,498	37,850	44,560

Source: Committee to Review, *Progress Report*, 1977, Table 4.6, p. 21.

remuneration). That right, however, is not laid down in law. Company law merely proscribes that directors act in the best interests of the company; this has been translated into the requirement that directors act in the best interests of the owners (shareholders) of the company.[20] There was (and still is) nothing in corporate law to suggest that owning equity incurs responsibility for the management of the company.

The dilution of ownership, and the absence of legally binding definitions of ownership responsibility, created strong disincentives for shareholders to assume ownership responsibilities. Where there is no clear owner and no responsibility laid down in law, there is no clear duty on any one individual or institution to assume ownership responsibility.[21] Institutional owners moreover were 'primarily responsible to the person whose savings are entrusted to its care'.[22] Their primary responsibility was to savers rather than to borrowers.[23] Financial institutions had a primary responsibility to those who channelled their savings into their funds. 'The objective of a pension fund is to maximise the rate of return by investments',[24] whilst that of the insurance companies was 'to ensure that at all times the funds will be able to meet liabilities to policy holders and their reasonable expectations'.[25]

In theory, owners could influence management by expressing either exit or voice. The principal may express exit by selling shares in the company or exercise voice by expressing concerns to management with a view to influencing an improvement in the company's performance.[26] The structure of ownership, the absence of legally binding requirements of responsibility and the obligation of institutions to maximise the savings they controlled created major disincentives for any institutional shareholder to exercise voice. Rational behaviour for such institutions was to maximise income streams (dividend returns) and asset values (share prices) by share trading to guarantee the best possible income stream and to enhance their asset values. It is for this reason that observers have characterised shareholding in this country as being dominated by residual and property rights: the right to the residual income of the company and the right to trade shares to maximise their income.[27] The financial institutions had strong financial interests in the right to accrue income both from dividend returns and from trading in company securities, not least since by the late 1960s, company securities accounted for the major part of the distribution of their funds (Table 4.2). This, when combined with the free rider constraints on intervening which followed from diluted ownership, meant that the financial institutions had no real incentive to intervene in the affairs of individual companies. Rather the incentive is to exercise the right to transfer property rights in shares – by off-loading shares in under-performing companies on the stock exchange.

The financial institutions had little real incentive to assist the Labour Government in realising its objectives for industry – if that meant active

Table 4.2 Distribution of pension and insurance funds at market value

Percentage distribution of new investment

	Insurance companies		Pension funds
	Long term funds 1966–1970	General Funds 1966–1970	All funds 1966–1970
Public sector securities	16	–13	3
Company securities	40	75	70
Loans and mortgages	20	10	1
Property	20	–6	19
Short term and other assets	4	34	7
Total	100	100	100
Market value (£ million)	716 pa	57 pa	533 pa

Source: Committee to Review, *Progress Report*, Table 4.7, p. 23 and Table 4.8, p. 24.

Notes: The general funds of the insurance companies relate to non-life funds which face liabilities which are more short term and less predictable than those of life funds.

involvement in industry and any lessening of their rights to maximise income from dividends and share trading. The legacy of mutual suspicion if not outright hostility between the leading financial institutions and key members of the new Labour Government did not help matters. Wilson himself had described the City of London as being characterised by a 'casino mentality' and had referred to the Stock Exchange as a 'spivs' paradise' in the 1958 election campaign – remarks hardly likely to create the basis for constructive co-operative relations between his new Government and the City.[28]

Finally, any bargaining between the City institutions and the Government in relation to the exercise of ownership responsibilities was always to be constrained by mutual suspicion, and the extent to which the City believed there was a credible threat of enhanced regulation of its activities by Government.[29] This in turn was determined however by bargaining leverages between the City over the Government. In the 1960s, the City had greater bargaining leverage than the Government. This derived from the Government's need to maintain City confidence against a background of balance of payments deficits and exchange rate problems and Wilson's determination to avoid Devaluation at all costs.[30]

The alternative route to realising the objectives of structural change and effective management was to promote take-overs. Critics of the Anglo-American system have argued that rights to the residual have always dominated the behaviour of shareholders in this country.[31] The system is believed to encourage owners to treat equity as assets that can be transferred to other owners (and hence the stock market becomes a market in property rights) that in turn encourage managerial failure to be corrected through a market for corporate control.[32]

Takeover bids had existed before the Second World War, but they had received great impetus in the 1950s.[33] The decision of the Conservative Government in 1958 and 1959 to hand over regulation to City practitioners ensured 'the least restrictive form of regulatory regime' based on a voluntary code of conduct and, as such, provided a regulatory framework which eased rather than constrained the potential for take-over bids.[34] It is not surprising then that the mid 1960s became a period of intense take-over activity.[35] For the Wilson Government, however, the dilemma was that the take-over route would encourage a behavioural pattern it abhorred: where equity ownership is conducted in property rights terms, where ownership may be transferred at any point in time to the highest bidder and where the principal, seeking to maximise income and asset values, transfers ownership of equity into shares promising the highest returns.

The tension lay in devising a means of persuading shareholders to effect structural change and impose effective management on industry whilst avoiding the 'casino' of property rights behaviour with the ultimate objective of producing world-class industries capable of competing in the global markets. The Government had thus set itself an agenda of reforming corporate governance without alienating the financial markets or unleashing a 'spivs' paradise'.

III

The solutions the Government adopted had the potential to transform relations between the company and its numerous stakeholders and thus transform corporate governance in this country. It chose two approaches a) by supporting mergers and take-overs – the active monitoring route and b) by changing the nature of governance – the indirect or administrative route. In both, the aim was to create large firms directed by modern management guided by enlightened views of their relations with all stakeholders. Of the two, the latter involved the more fundamental, and potentially more radical, route to modernising the firm. This route, however, was administratively complicated, legally complex and hence time consuming. The account of the administrative solution and its demise is one of missed opportunity to reform corporate governance.

The Government's indirect solution to the reformation of shareholder behaviour was to engage it in a major re-think of the role of the firm in modern society and its relations with all its stakeholders. In this section we assess the attempt to re-think the role of the firm and its relations with stakeholders as well as the Government's attempts to reform shareholder behaviour. The most striking aspect of the analysis of contemporary government archives from these years is that in so many ways, the ideas pursued by 'Old' Labour of the late 1960s, anticipated those of 'New' Labour today and pre-empt many of the issues currently being pursued in the attempt to 'modernise' the UK economy. Of these, 'Old' Labour's desire to re-think the role of the firm in modern society is particularly striking. Stake holding is not 'new'. The idea, if not the exact terminology, was very much under discussion in the mid 1960s.

A momentum grew within government circles, prompted by the activities of the Board of Trade, to address explicitly what role the firm should adopt and how it could maximise performance, and hence international competi-tiveness, by reforming its relations with its myriad stakeholders. The issue was first raised in November 1966 in a proposal from the Board of Trade to the Department of Economic Affairs that, as well as pressing on with work on a Second Companies Bill dealing with 'those recommendations of the Jenkins Committee which have not been dealt with in the present Bill, consideration should be given to philosophical but more fundamen-tal questions on the operation of companies'.[36] Long-run success, it was argued, derived from a re-thinking of these relationships in a wider agenda to reform management and to re-channel the objectives of industry. Profit maximisation was crucial, but it was to be combined with and channelled by optimal relations between all stakeholders, namely shareholders, workers, suppliers, customers and managers.

By the beginning of December 1966, a working party had been formed consisting of officials from the Board of Trade (who chaired the meetings), the Department of Economic Affairs, the Ministry of Labour, the Inland Revenue, the Treasury and the Ministry of Technology.[37] The 'fundamental questions' vexing ministers' minds concerned the relation of the company with its shareholders, the State, its suppliers and employees. The starting point was 'there is no agreement on what should be the aims and respon-sibilities of companies and what needs to be done to see that they are car-ried out'.[38] The working party considered whether 'there (should) be any representation of the public interest in addition to (and reinforcing) that of shareholders in the process of making boards of directors account for the performance, in the widest sense, of their companies' and whether Govern-ment 'should rely on the voluntary co-operation of companies' or whether 'it should induce companies by fiscal and other incentive, or impose legal obligations on companies, to carry out policies which it conceives to be in the national interest'.[39] Supplier and employee stake-holding were consid-ered in terms of the right to information of the latter and potential exploita-tion of large customers by companies (and vice versa). These are modern questions about the stakeholder firm: but were written over thirty years ago.

This raised issues on the role of the shareholder. Three issues were identified as crucial: the need to define the role and responsibilities of the shareholders, the accountability of management, and the appointment of management. In relation to the first issue, that of the role and responsibilities of shareholders, four problem areas were identified: what control the shareholders should have over managers, whether shareholder power should be strengthened and, if so, how, and whether institutional shareholders should be encouraged to take a more active part in controlling the management of the companies in which they invest. These are modern issues, which were to re-surface in the Cadbury report several decades later.[40]

The discussions quickly focused on the role of non-executive directors and how their role could be strengthened. Officials were keen to see an enhancement of the powers of non-voting shareholders and considered the abolition of non-voting shares. Officials also wanted company performance, policy and practice to be opened up to wider public scrutiny: almost a name and shame approach. To this effect they considered the relaxation of libel laws so as to permit more press analysis and criticism.

The views submitted to the commission on company law reform, however, were still relevant. The predicament was that one could not legislate for the 'right' people to do the 'right' thing. Value judgements were not easy to define in legal terms. Officials were reluctantly to come to the decision that: 'the value of any director can only be decided by the boards of directors concerned and in theory by the shareholders who elect them. It is difficult to see how the law can intervene effectively in value judgements of this kind'.[41]

Ultimately, the working party was to conclude that the problem was not one for Government to legislate for, but for the City to deal with since 'if only the City would put the right people on boards, they could do a lot to counter the self-perpetuating oligarchies . . . (But) too often the people appointed are . . . purely financial and, what is worse, unimaginatively financial . . .'.[42] Although more active participation by institutional shareholders was warranted, the Working Party was to conclude that it was difficult to see how this could be enforced.[43] Equally, it was argued that it was difficult to see how the law could intervene effectively in value judgements on executive directors. The requirement was not for more legislation on duties, but that directors understand their duties since 'In the companies court and in practice at the Bar, the impression is gained that directors are generally not only unaware of their fiduciary duties but are also little aware of any of their duties at all . . .'.[44]

As discussions became embroiled in the legal technicalities of defining how one might legislate for the 'right' people to do the 'right' thing, the Government increasingly turned to another and superficially easier way of influencing stakeholder relations. The role of the shareholder within such stake-holding relations was crucial. The Government increasingly came to focus away from the behaviour of all stakeholder groups and value judgements, to a re-thinking of what shareholding actually entailed: the first time that the state had seriously considered the rights and responsibilities of shareholding. This thinking derived from the DEA and prompted attempts to address explicitly what rights and responsibilities shareholding entailed.

The agenda looked to neither the legal process nor the operation of the financial markets, but rather considered how governance could be reformed via the influence of government as a shareholder and was based on the realisation that the state had acquired by default shares in many companies, not as a result of deliberate policy but through a series of events over the years. By the mid 1960s, departmental responsibility for government shareholdings was widely spread among different departments. In most cases the shareholder was the sponsor department for the industry concerned. But Government had two distinct interests as a shareholder in a private firm: in the general welfare of the industry to which the firm belonged and in the performance of the firm itself.

The first was termed the 'industrial' and the second the 'propertorial' or 'shareholder' interest.[45] 'Propertorial' interest was defined in exchequer and efficiency terms with efficiency defined as rates of return on capital and the raising of capital.[46] The Treasury believed it should be both shareholder and arbiter of the aims of the companies it 'controlled'. The Treasury argued that propertorial interest meant it should act as the 'shareholder' department. It further maintained that shareholding was to be measured and executed in the strictly financial terms of the company in question and 'effective management' of equity. This stance led to outright opposition from most other departments: 'one argument against giving the Treasury (these) functions was that the companies concerned would almost inevitably get a raw deal as a result, because the Treasury's reaction to any proposal to spend money was to oppose it'.[47]

In contrast, shareholding for the spending departments soon meant the use of equity holdings to give government a dominant position in a given industry, and thus to set the competitive agenda. In inter-departmental meetings, the 'battle' between the Treasury and the other departments for control continued with no real conclusion. This persuaded the spending departments to pursue their own agenda: in the war of attrition, the conflict between the views of the Treasury and the spending departments was leading nowhere. Other departments increasingly focused on questions of ownership responsibility: who (and in what sense) was responsible for the shares owned by government, how did government interpret its ownership responsibilities and how might that ownership be used to influence the behaviour of other shareholders.

The impetus behind these moves derived from growing realisation of the extent to which Government had become a shareholder in its own right. The line of causation led not from an explicit (or implicit) desire to increase public ownership but rather from a growing awareness of the extent of government shareholding and a questioning of what duties and responsibilities the shareholding entailed.[48] These implications included the rights and responsibilities of Government as shareholder. Rights included the rights to a proportionate share in the future profits of the company, a proportionate share in the company's net assets if the company should be liquidated, and a proportionate vote on any major changes in the company, as well as the right to nominate one or more directors and to approval of significant amendments to the company's activities or any alteration of rights attached to existing shares. These are the standard rights of share-ownership.

But in addition proposals emerged to enhance the Government's rights to 'influence the policies of companies in which they have a shareholding . . .', in line with current incomes, prices or industrial policy as well as the argument that Government shareholding should be used to 'ensure that companies in which they have a shareholding are run efficiently and profitably'.[49] Ownership was to entail explicit responsibilities on the part of the owners to the company in question. At this point, there was no explicit objective of increasing Government shareholding in order to influence company efficiency and profitability. Nor did discussions move beyond the basic principle to the mechanics of making those responsibilities operational. By this time, the impetus had turned to a more direct way of influencing the structure of industry and the quality of management.

Initiatives to re-think the responsibilities of shareholding and the role of the firm in modern society involved philosophical discussions on the nature of the firm, the definition of 'right' and the interpretation of 'ownership'. Not surprisingly, discussion of abstract ideals became problematic, especially since they involved conflict between departments and the intractable issue of defining such ideals in legislative terms. The move away from the 'administrative' solution was determined in large part by the philosophical problems involved in legislating for abstract ideals, but also by a sense that such moves required a long-term perspective. Legislating for what amounted to a cultural change in the way shareholders behaved required reformation of company law: something most governments shy away from. Company law is not an issue which wins the hearts and minds of voters, it is however an issue which could consume much valuable parliamentary (and civil service) time. It is not surprising then that the Wilson Government should cede to an aversion to a time-consuming administrative minefield, which promised little electoral return and should turn instead to more immediate methods of influencing the structure of industry and the quality of its management.

IV

Alongside the abstract, but 'new' and fundamental discussions, the Wilson Government engaged in a direct attempt to effect technological innovation by directly influencing the structure and management of British industry. By 1967 the emphasis had moved away from the abstract to the direct intervention. The mechanism was not reformation of existing legislation or the creation of new company law, but rather a new institution, The Industrial Reorganisation Corporation (IRC), which was assigned the explicit task of promoting rationalisation and of identifying areas requiring special assistance.[50] The guiding ethos was not to nationalise but to rationalise, and to intervene when and where markets did not work.

Gentle persuasion characterised the first twelve months of the IRC's existence. In its first months of operation, the IRC limited its activities to a 'soft sell' approach, of 'persuading firms to undertake voluntary mergers, backed by judicious offers of financial support on attractive terms'.[51] The emphasis was on advice, gentle persuasion and the offer of development loans as a financial incentive to merger. By the end of the summer of 1966, however, the EDC had reached the general conclusion that persuasion alone was insufficient to bring about the necessary rationalisation. Persuasion had failed to convince either the 'City' or managers in industry that rationalisation was in their and the country's best interests: the 'soft sell approach does not always produce results as quickly as they (IRC) would like or the country's economic position requires'.[52] As a result, the IRC began to press for a more assertive role, the definition of assertion being 'supporting particular companies in a programme of acquisition, if necessary through contested takeovers'.[53]

The Government now decided on a pro-active policy designed to achieve its objectives.[54] Intervention to promote acquisition was to be guided by 'support for management strong enough to do the job or where necessary the injection of management from outside'.[55] This was an explicit acknowledgement that resolution of the managerial problem could not be left to the markets. Corporate governance mechanisms were unable (or unwilling) to exercise ownership responsibilities and, as such, an outside body was needed to instigate change. In deciding on such a course, the Government unwittingly was to set itself on course for a confrontation with the 'markets' and to influence decisively the development of corporate governance in this country.

The activities of the IRC are examined in this paper and in the context of the evolution of corporate governance, by reference to its participation in three take-overs, each of which marked a signal change in the evolution of strategy. Each brought the Government more into direct play and potential conflict with the markets and was ultimately to have serious and lasting effects on corporate governance in this country. The first take-over dates from the autumn of 1967 as the IRC publicly and actively backed GEC's bid for AEI. The early summer of 1968 marked another switch as the IRC actively intervened in the markets to ensure the success of Kent's bid for Cambridge Instruments. The third again dated from the summer of 1968 when the IRC backed one party in a contested take-over bid. In a two-year period, policy had moved from gentle persuasion, to public backing, to active (but supposedly secret) intervention in the markets and to active and public support by government in a contested take-over bid.

It is not surprising that the electrical engineering and electronics industry became the focus of attention: it comprised modern growth industries, which 'employ a large proportion of the UK's scarce resources of scientists, engineers and technicians and are engaged in many activities which have a direct and fundamental effect on the country's economic growth and its balance of payments'.[56] But the record of exports and productivity growth were variously described as 'slow', 'poor' and 'problematic'. Both, as such, were deserving of attention since 'even a slight improvement in their productivity is worth much effort to achieve'.[57]

In 1965 the National Plan recorded the industry's own belief 'that continued technological progress depends on sufficient profitability to obtain funds for research and development and to justify the raising of capital to increase the scale and efficiency of production. These matters in turn are closely involved in such questions as the most rational structure of the industry ...'.[58] Government was to claim that in view of the increasing scale of manufacturing operations on the Continent, the process of major structural change towards consolidation in the British industry can by no means be considered complete. Three years later, the situation had not changed. The IRC argued for 'changes in industrial structure' which could 'effect more than a slight improvement (in productivity)'.[59]

In 1966, there were eleven major firms in the electrical and electronics industry. Declining profit margins and return on capital employed between 1965 and 1968 were symptomatic of the industry's inefficiencies (Table 4.3). But there were also wide variations between different firms with profit margins ranging from in excess of 10 per cent by GEC, DECCA and EMI to less than 4 per cent at Hawker Siddeley, ICL and AEI.

Detailed evaluation of the companies in the industry by the Board of Trade and the DEA identified candidates for potential merger in terms of product-mix and managerial performance. Product-mix criteria stressed compatibility of products by companies, the rationale being to promote horizontal merger rather than merger between companies with non-like products. This, of course, was to raise questions of monopoly power. The Government line, however, was that the objective was to create companies able to compete internationally. The global not the domestic market was the arena in which such companies were to operate.

Table 4.3 The Performance of the Electrical Industry

Company	Latest Year End	Year	Sales £m	Net Profit Before Tax £m	Profit Margin %	Return on Capital Employed
AEI		1966			1.93	
		1965			3.27	
Plessey	Jun–30	1967	145	13.83	9.54	15.30
		1966	128	12.09	9.45	13.40
		1965	105	15.19	14.47	22.20
English Electric	Dec–31	1967	412	19.99	4.85	9.00
		1966	291	16.48	5.66	13.00
		1965	245	13.97	5.70	12.60
GEC (GEC & AEI for 3 mths '68)	Mar–31	1968	257	18.65	7.26	6.90
		1967	180	17.73	9.85	17.00
		1966	169	19.46	11.51	19.80
Hawker Siddeley	Dec–31	1967	358	11.73	3.28	7.00
		1966	384	12.91	3.36	7.80
		1965	381	11.91	3.13	7.90
BICC	Dec–31	1967	293	19.49	6.65	13.90
		1966	299	21.62	7.23	16.90
		1965	254	18.59	7.32	15.70
Thorn	Mar–31	1968	176	14.85	8.44	17.20
		1967	na	10.30	na	16.00
		1966	na	10.42	na	17.60
Reyrolls/ Parsons	Dec–31	1967	na	5.50	na	6.10
		1966	na	5.33	na	16.90
		1965	na	5.20	na	17.50
ICL	Sep–30	1967	67	3.03	4.52	6.60
		1966	63	2.33	3.70	7.50
		1965	55	–0.51	–0.93	na
Ferranti	Mar–31	1968	na	2.82	na	16.60
		1967	na	3.12	na	19.50
		1966	na	2.74	na	17.90
EMI	Jun–30	1967	107	10.43	9.75	21.20
		1966	103	11.25	26.30	24.70
		1965	100	10.22	10.22	26.30
DECCA	Mar–31	1967	40	4.47	11.18	25.00
		1966	36	4.32	12.00	25.40
		1965	37	3.94	10.65	24.50

Source: *The Stock Exchange Gazette*, Market Surveys, 1965–1968 inclusive and EW 26/69: Appendix II.

The other and in many respects determining feature was the relative managerial strengths of the companies. Government archives detail how AEI's disappointing sales and profit record were attributed to product exposure, financial weakness and weak top management. The three were seen as inter-related. Product exposure was traced to expansion in capacity and a concentration in the heavy sector of electrical engineering. Product exposure was interpreted as the outcome of misguided management strategy. Financial weakness in turn was linked to the inability of management to implement financial management and control.[60]

Similar criticisms were levelled at English Electric and Cambridge Instruments. Government archives show that ministers and officials believed that although English Electric was 'basically well-managed and technologically second to very few in its field', it lacked the 'drive and bite of GEC in its leadership and has too much fat in its middle management layer'.[61] Company profits at Cambridge Instruments had been declining because of short production runs and one off jobs; the company's profits had been declining. Although new management had been brought in to rationalise the company's production methods, City commentators and politicians alike felt that the 'fruits of this modernisation are slow in appearing'.[62]

Is there any evidence to suggest that shareholders shared the Government's misgivings about the management and performance of these companies? What is lacking in the standard analyses of the mergers and takeovers of the 1960s is any attempt to analyse the behaviour of individual institutional investors.[63] In this and the following section we use a variety of financial data to explore that behaviour. We used four pieces of evidence to evaluate shareholder reaction to the performance of GEC, AEI and English Electric to see whether named institutions put any pressure on management. The first is City comment and evaluation: this reflected current thinking in the City and was used by current and potential investors to assist their trading decisions. For this we used the regular share ratings survey produced by *The Stock Exchange Gazette* – a quarterly survey that summarised City evaluation of companies within given sectors – together with qualitative assessment in the financial press.

Shares in electrical firms were never seen as being 'outstanding buys', but the financial press rated them as being worthwhile investments and certainly worth holding on to. In 1967, City comment still 'sung the merits'[64] and envisaged the future prosperity of an independent AEI.[65] English Electric's acquisitions and rationalisations were said to 'augur well for the future'.[66] Until October 1965, AEI, English Electric and GEC were deemed in the share rating evaluation as worthwhile investments, and even after that date, as shares to hold on to (Table 4.4). It is significant that the market did not pick out any one of these companies as being higher rated than its competitors. Only Thorn and Ever Ready in this group were ever deemed, during this period, as having 'little to go for'.

Table 4.4 Electrical Industry: Share Rating

	Jan– 65	Apr– 65	Jul– 65	Oct– 65	Jan– 66	Apr– 66	Jul– 66	Oct– 66	Jan– 67	Apr– 67
AEI	***	***	***	**	**	**	**	**	**	**
BICC	***	***	***	**	**	**	**	**	**	**
DECCA	***	***	**	**	**	**	**	**	**	**
EMI	***	***	**	**	**	**	**	**	***	**
Eliott	***	***	**	**	**	**	**	**	**	**
Eng Electric	***	***	***	**	**	**	**	**	**	**
Ever Ready	***	**	**	**	**	**	**	**	**	*
GEC	***	***	**	**	**	**	**	**	**	**
ICC	**	**	**	**	**	**	**	**	**	**
Reyrolle	***	***	***	**	**	**	**	**	**	**
Plessey	***	**	**	**	***	**	**	**	***	**
Thorn	***	***	**	**	**	**	*	**	**	*

Source: *Stock Exchange Gazette.*

Key:

**** A recommended buy
*** A worthwhile investment;
** A share to hold;
* Little to go for

The second piece of evidence relates to dividend yields and the price-earnings ratio. Investors, looking for a favourable return on equity, would compare AEI, GEC and English Electric with those of their rivals. From the mid 1960s, the *Stock Exchange Gazette* provided actual and potential investors with quarterly surveys of share returns by industrial sector. For investors concerned with immediate returns, the dividend yield was the salient figure. Throughout the period reviewed, AEI was one of the top-rated industries in the electrical sector, recording above average dividend yields in each quarter (Table 4.5). English Electric scored well, only performing below average in two quarters (July and October 1966). General Electric, in stark contrast, was not viewed as one of the better securities: its dividend yield in each quarter was below that of the average. For investors looking for immediate returns, English Electric and AEI promised good returns: GEC, less so.

For those looking for long-term investment, the price-earnings ratio was the important figure. Again, we used data compiled from the quarterly surveys produced by the *Stock Exchange Gazette* (Table 4.6). These results indicate a degree of uncertainty in relation to AEI, English Electric and GEC, when compared to other companies in the electrical industry. Up to October 1966, AEI had a higher than average price-earnings ratio. English Electric and GEC, by comparison, were regularly below average. If the markets believed the immediate returns of AEI, English Electric and GEC

Table 4.5 Electrical Industry: Dividend Yields

	Jan–65	Apr–65	Jul–65	Oct–65	Jan–66	Apr–66	Jul–66	Oct–66	Jan–67	Apr–67
AEI	5.00	4.90	5.30	5.00	4.80	5.00	5.00	6.7	6.90	6.70
BICC	4.30	4.60	5.00	4.50	4.70	5.00	4.80	5.6	5.20	4.90
DECCA	4.20	4.50	5.10	4.70	4.40	4.20	3.70	4.30	4.10	3.90
EMI	5.00	5.60	na	6.30	5.60	4.90	4.70	5.50	5.60	4.90
Eliott	2.60	3.10	na	3.90	4.30	4.50	4.50	5.10	4.80	4.50
Eng Electric	4.60	5.00	5.30	4.50	4.40	4.50	4.30	5.2	5.00	5.00
Ever Ready	3.70	4.00	na	3.90	3.80	4.00	4.00	4.7	4.80	4.20
GEC	3.60	3.70	4.20	4.10	4.20	4.10	3.70	4.70	4.40	4.30
ICC	4.70	5.20	6.70	7.20	6.00	6.20	4.90	5.5	5.10	4.60
Reyrolle	3.90	3.70	3.70	3.50	3.60	3.30	4.80	5.9	4.10	6.50
Plessey	3.80	3.70	na	4.10	4.20	4.50	4.20	5.8	5.50	5.10
Thorn	1.90	2.10	na	2.70	2.60	2.80	2.40	2.9	2.90	2.40
Media	4.05	4.25	5.10	4.30	4.35	4.50	4.40	5.35	4.90	4.75

Source: Stock Exchange Gazette.

Note: the dividend yield is the dividend payable per share expressed as a percentage of the market price per share. This ratio reflects the stock market's views of the *current* expectations of the company.

Table 4.6 Electrical Industry: Price-Earnings Ratios

	Jan–65	Apr–65	Jul–65	Oct–65	Jan–66	Apr–66	Jul–66	Oct–66	Jan–67	Apr–67
AEI	23.70	13.90	12.80	13.70	14.10	16.20	14.40	10.50	10.30	14.90
BICC	20.00	12.70	10.20	13.50	13.60	12.50	13.10	12.50	13.70	12.90
DECCA	21.10	16.30	na	11.50	11.90	12.70	13.80	14.10	14.60	15.90
EMI	14.20	11.00	na	11.80	13.60	15.10	15.30	11.50	12.10	13.90
Eliott	26.60	25.20	na	15.20	na	12.50	26.00	31.00	36.00	38.50
Eng Electric	16.20	11.90	11.20	14.70	14.90	11.40	12.60	12.50	13.10	13.20
Ever Ready	18.30	15.00	na	13.60	13.90	12.90	14.00	12.10	11.80	13.40
GEC	21.40	12.20	11.40	11.50	12.30	12.50	13.40	10.50	11.30	11.70
ICC	19.10	16.30	na	na	na	na	na	na	17.80	19.70
Reyrolle	19.80	10.50	na	11.50	11.40	11.90	10.30	8.80	9.10	8.30
Plessey	17.70	15.30	na	13.90	13.30	12.10	13.40	14.40	14.80	15.80
Thorn	18.60	10.10	na	11.50	11.60	10.90	13.00	14.50	14.60	18.00
Media	19.45	13.30	11.30	13.50	13.45	12.50	13.40	12.50	13.40	14.40

Source: Stock Exchange Gazette.

Notes: The price-earnings ratio is the market price of an equity share divided by earnings per share. This ratio reflects the stock market's expectations of the *future* earnings of the company. The higher the number, the greater the expectations.

were good, they were far less convinced in terms of future prospects. Other companies in the electrical industry promised better long-term investment.

Market prices reflect the sum of all share transactions. Had shareholders believed other companies promised better immediate and/or future returns, they would sell shares: the property rights hypothesis whereby equity is sold to the highest bidder. The third piece of evidence is that of the share price. The evidence (Figure 4.1) suggests property rights behaviour in the case of AEI from March 1967 as the market price fell, albeit there was some recovery from August 1967. Share prices for English Electric in contrast were relatively stable until August 1967, after which time the price increased substantially. The market price for GEC, again in contrast, was always higher than that for English Electric and AEI, and increased substantially from June 1967.

Is this prima facie evidence of the markets expressing disquiet about AEI and switching funds to a more profitable investment, namely GEC? Market prices reflect the sum of all transactions. They do not enable us to identify the transacting parties – or the number of shares each party bought or sold. In order to do so, we used the fourth source of evidence: the annual registers of shareholders all publicly quoted companies, by law, are required to keep. These tell us who owned shares, how many shares they held, and whether they bought or sold shares. In line with the general pattern of shareholding in UK companies, the distribution of shareholding in AEI had seen a steady increase in the share held by the insurance companies, pension funds and banks since 1950, and a weakening in the share of those held by private individuals (Table 4.7).

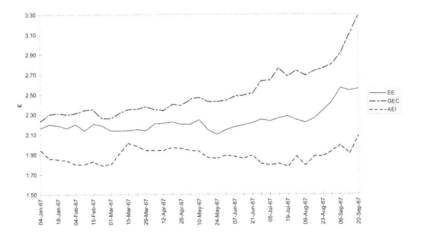

Figure 4.1 Market Price per share in 1967

Source: Stock Exchange Gazette.

Table 4.7 AEI: Stockholdings: Percent of holding by value

	Insurance Companies	Investment Trusts	Pension Trusts	Banks and other nominee companies	Other Limited Companies	Individual members	Total
1950	7.84	3.22	0.29	9.63	41.49	37.53	100
1955	23.10	5.87	2.27	15.78	2.01	50.97	100
1960	17.85	4.37	2.50	15.44	7.19	52.65	100
1963	17.74	4.68	3.91	16.60	6.84	50.23	100
1964	18.33	5.03	4.23	16.11	7.17	49.13	100
1965	18.91	5.07	4.56	16.70	6.68	48.08	100
1966	19.32	5.99	4.91	16.80	6.75	46.23	100

Source: AEI, Annual Report and Accounts.

Was there any sense of shareholders exercising property rights by selling their holdings? Our analysis of the share registers of the company (Table 4.8) suggests that shareholders did not sell shares. Indeed, the evidence indicates the contrary, with many of the principle shareholders buying AEI shares. Amongst the major shareholders, the Co-Op, the Prudential, Royal Insurance, Equity and Law Life, Norwich Union, Sun Life Canada and Union Pension all increased their holdings. Other major shareholders neither sold nor bought: this group includes Scottish Amicable, Sun Life Insurance, Royal London Mutual, and Legal and General.

One could interpret this evidence as an absence by the financial institutions of property rights behaviour. It would certainly indicate an absence of 'exit' pressure on AEI. There is, however, an alternative explanation: the financial institutions, having regard to the declared objectives of the Economic Development Council and the IRC, had good cause to believe merger or take-over likely, in which case they would find their asset values increased if and when either took place.[67] The markets were expressing neither voice nor exit: they were behaving not in a manner which best protected the interests of the company, but in a manner which best protected their declared objectives of protecting the savings channelled into their funds.

A similar story emerges from our analysis of the share registers of English Electric (Table 4.9). There is little evidence of exit behaviour from the major institutional shareholders of that company. On the contrary, there is evidence of a propensity to increase holdings: as evidenced by the purchases of shares made by the Prudential, the Co-Op, the Pension Fund, London RBS Nominees and Unilever. Here the evidence is one of 'old' and 'new' institutions acquiring shares – presumably on the expectation of enhanced asset values if and when take-over bids ensued.

Table 4.8 Number of AEI Shares Held by Financial Institutions (listed in descending order by number of shares held in 1967)

	14-May–65	15-Apr–66	14-Apr–67
Prudential	2,045,233	2,045,433	2,048,725
Co-Op	389,949	449,199	509,199
Pearl Assurance	500,160	500,160	500,160
Norwich Union	432,832	432,832	491,832
Royal London Mutual	458,570	458,570	458,570
Legal & General	365,000	365,000	365,000
Pension Fund Securities	347,500	347,500	362,500
London Office RBS Nominees	366,577	331,386	350,596
Royal Insurance	276,916	276,916	286,916
Refuge Assurance	209,712	209,712	237,712
Sun Life Canada	217,333	194,833	234,833
Union Pension	120,000	134,000	150,000
North Assurance	137,000	147,000	147,000
Scottish Widows	140,111	140,111	140,111
Shell Mex Pensions	58,000	96,000	137,615
Sun Life Insurance	137,455	137,455	137,455
Equity & Law Life	100,000	100,000	130,000
Commercial Union	125,264	125,394	125,394
Scottish Amicable	120,000	120,000	120,000
Scottish Union	90,000	100,000	110,000
Scottish Provident	92,500	100,000	100,000
Princes Street Nominees	77,959	85,749	96,933
London Assurance	95,000	95,000	95,000
London Life	88,610	88,594	88,782
Eagle Star	72,568	69,568	72,478
Scottish American Investment	20,260	30,000	70,000
Textile Pensions	60,291	65,000	65,000
Mercantile & General	62,000	62,000	62,000
Lon & Liverpool Globe	20,000	20,000	60,000
Scottish Mutual	60,000	60,000	60,000
Sun Insurance	60,259	55,898	55,898
Ocean Accident	53,000	53,920	53,920
United Friendly	39,551	39,551	39,551
Royal Exchange	71,906	39,100	35,200
PAT Pensions	33,333	33,333	33,333
Life Assoc of Scotland	25,960	25,960	25,960
Union Provident	15,000	15,000	25,000
Standard Trust	24,000	24,000	24,000
Embankment Trust	9,000	20,000	20,000
1928	20,000	20,000	20,000
Unilever	17,500	17,500	20,000
Fenchurch Nominees	28,357	25,454	19,929
North American Trust	14,840	14,840	16,880
London Ass Nominees	9,500	9,500	10,125
Lombard Street Nominees	14,863	9,713	8,838
UK Temperance	60,000	60,000	200
Scottish Life	38,600	38,600	0

Source: AEI, Annual Register of Share Registers, Companies House, London.

Table 4.9 Institutional Shareholding (Number of Shares) in English Electric

	No. of shares 1966	No. of shares 1967	No. of shares 1968	Percentage of Ordinary Equity in 1968
Prudential	1,870,082	2,245,018	3,283,635	7.56
Co-Op	343,592	412,310	878,873	2.02
Pension Fund	356,500	427,800	789,500	1.82
London R.B.S. Nominees	399,798	542,308	672,010	1.55
Unilever	0	10,800	499,700	1.15
Pearl	224,130	268,956	456,286	1.05
Commercial Union	140,495	183,066	442,550	1.02
Norwich Ass	242,448	236,937	355,112	0.82
Scottish Widows	214,392	257,270	319,774	0.74
Equity and Law	180,000	216,000	294,766	0.68
UK Temperance	125,000	150,000	281,722	0.65
Prudential Nominees	138,234	165,880	237,632	0.55
London & Manchester	1,472	2,816	233,552	0.54
Scottish Provident	110,000	132,000	230,000	0.53
Refuge	27,954	33,544	178,754	0.41
Eagle Star	14,400	20,131	178,331	0.41
Sun Life Assurance	86,750	120,000	170,187	0.39
Mercantile & General	77,500	93,000	149,000	0.34

Source: English Electric, Annual Register of Share Registers, Companies House, London.
Notes: Total number of ordinary shares in 1968 = 43,428,595

Examination of the share registers for both companies indicates that 'City' institutions did not pursue exit behaviour. Exit behaviour, such as it was, derived from individual and industry investors. There was no sense of AEI or English Electric management being under pressure from the markets to improve the company's performance. Share prices and share transactions suggest the markets did not believe such pressure appropriate. On the contrary, the growth in share prices and the propensity of institutional shareholders to increase their shares suggest the markets put a high premium on their equity holdings in both companies.

Our four pieces of evidence (market comment and evaluation, accounting ratios, share prices and share transactions) indicate that the financial institutions did not put any exit pressure on either AEI or English Electric to improve performance. On the contrary, our evidence suggests that the markets fulfilled their primary objective of best protecting and maximising the returns on their investments. The behaviour indicates that the financial institutions had good reason to believe a good return on their decision to retain equity holdings in these companies. Weak profit performances by those companies seen in isolation might question such beliefs. The markets self evidently had good reason to believe holding on to their holdings (and even in some cases increasing them) was the rational move. What made them take such a view was, of course, the policy agenda pursued by the Government.

V

In this section we explore the involvement of the IRC in three take-over bids. Standard analyses of the takeovers have not been informed by either of our two primary sources of information. First, the government archives we use on these takeovers have only recently become available. Second, standard analyses have never used share registers, despite the wealth of information they contain on differential behaviour by named institutions. As in the previous section we use the share register information, but now combine it with government archives to identify institutional shareholder behaviour.

Explicit Government support for mergers and takeovers via the IRC prompted take-over bids: of £120m by GEC for AEI (27 September 1967), by Rank for Cambridge Instruments (6 May 1968) and by Plessey for English Electric (21 August 1968). One was not contested and succeeded (GEC for AEI); the other two were contested and failed.[68] Each of the three represents a key stage in the evolution of IRC policy and strategy. The first bid represented a new development in IRC policy: that of public support for a take-over bid. The third saw the IRC supporting one party over another in a contested bid. The second bid was in many respects the most revolutionary, in that it witnessed active intervention by the IRC in the markets to ensure the success of one party over another in a contested bid.

The GEC bid for AEI, so government archives reveal, was inspired not by GEC but by the IRC. In May 1967 the IRC approached Weinstock to discuss privately the reorganisation of the electrical industry and its future prospects. It transpired that the approach by the IRC had as its intention to propose the merger of the GEC and AEI.[69] Weinstock claimed that 'our first reaction was one of doubt mixed with a certain prejudice against the burden of reorganising what appeared to be a huge incompetent complex.'[70] A 'discreet' private dinner was held on 12 June 1967 between the IRC, Renwick (AEI), Keith (chief executive of Hill Samuel) and Latham of AEI to discuss the prospects for 'an arranged marriage'.[71] 'Latham and the AEI opposed such a marriage – as their feelings of opposition strengthened, so did the conviction of the IRC that a merger was a necessity.'[72] Weinstock meanwhile was cautious. Later he was to recall 'after further discussions and believing such an arrangement would not be to the detriment of our company, we agreed to effect such a merger'.[73] In practice, Weinstock needed little persuading – the issue was not whether he would mount a take-over bid, but when.[74]

The GEC bid for AEI was launched on 27 September 1967.[75] On 6 October the AEI Board announced their opposition to the bid since they 'did not believe that a merger of AEI and GEC was the best way of furthering the reorganisation of the electrical industry'.[76] Both Government (in the form of the Board of Trade, the DEA and MinTech) and the IRC favoured the take-over. Indeed, government archives indicate that GEC only made its bid 'after consultation with the Ministry of Technology and the Department of Economic Affairs'.[77] The merger promised the further rationalisation of the electrical engineering industry.[78] It also, and crucially, promised efficient management.[79] The crucial departure for the IRC was its initial approach to Weinstock to instigate the merger and the departure from its previous soft-sell strategy, to one of open support for the GEC bid. The strategy of open support for merger per se was very different from taking sides in battles between two parties.

The take-over battle for AEI ensued during the months of October and November 1967. From the company's share registers those who traded shares and thus benefited from the soaring market prices (Figure 4.2) can be identified.[80] The take-over battle was at its fiercest in October and November 1967 (Figure 4.2). Our research suggests that the 'old' financial institutions were not active participants. The bulk of the shares sold (and then bought) on the markets in October came from private individuals. Institutions sold only 130,398 shares.[81]

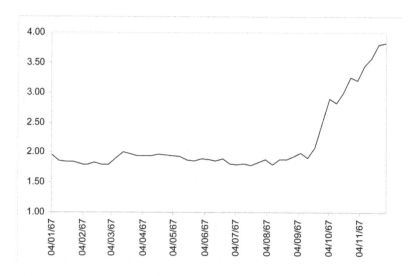

Figure 4.2 Share Prices for AEI during the 1967 Takeover Battle

Source: *Stock Exchange Gazette.*

In November, the 'new' City institutions of nominee, trustee, pension and investment companies dominated, with the nominee companies being particularly active, and thereby profiting from the escalation of AEI's share price. Here we have hard evidence from the primary sources that confirm the differential behaviour hypothesis. The 'old' institutions did not engage in share trading; the 'new' institutions, however, did.

How important was the public support of the IRC to GEC? Many observers believed it crucial and responsible for persuading many shareholders to accept GEC's offer.[82] But public support was not all the IRC did – it also, in the form of Kearton,[83] actively promoted the GEC bid by visiting important institutional shareholders to press them to support GEC. He did so because the Board of Trade had been warned of 'considerable resistance to the GEC bid' amongst institutional shareholders who 'had a basic sentiment against change'.[84] They were told it was their duty, 'in the national interest', to support the bid.[85] Our evidence suggests that they duly acquiesced. On 4 December 1967 AEI became a subsidiary of GEC.

The success of GEC's bid for AEI is important in three respects: first because the IRC initiated the merger, second because it represented the first time a Government agency had actively and publicly taken sides between two parties (in this case supporting GEC against the AEI board) and third, because it marked a turning point for major institutional investors. To declare itself openly in favour of one party was 'a development from (the IRC's) previously neutral role as a "midwife" in industrial restructuring'.[86] But in addition, by moving from that neutral role, the IRC had opposed the wishes of AEI's major institutional investors.[87]

This was not the victory of the private shareholder over the institutional shareholder, but that of the 'mass-market investment vehicles, unit and investment trusts and pension funds' over 'the insurance company establishment'.[88] It also marked the active intervention of the merchant bank establishment in the markets to ensure the success of a bid as Hill Samuel (which acted for GEC) engaged in heavy buying on the markets.[89] Insurance companies did not determine the fate of AEI: indeed the views of two of the major insurance companies (the Prudential and Pearl Assurance) counted for little in the face of IRC support for GEC which self evidently persuaded other institutional investors and the merchant banks in particular to engage in the frantic buying which ensured the success of GEC's bid. The lessons were crucial: aggressive buying by interested parties could guarantee success and the promise of enhanced asset values and future income streams.

The second stage in the evolution of IRC strategy came less than a year later. Growing concern at the activities (and manner) of the IRC reached crisis proportions in June 1968 with the involvement of the IRC in the contested bid for Cambridge Instruments. Cambridge Instruments produced industrial, medical and scientific research instruments for the scientific, medical and industrial markets that had over the years acquired a high reputation for the quality of its products. The company was a relatively large unit in a fragmented industry, employing by 1968 2,000 people (against an industry average of 500) and a turnover of about £4m (against an industry average of £1m). The company, however, had recorded several years of declining profits 'because of short production runs and one-off jobs'.[90]

On 6 May 1968 The Rank Organisation posted its formal offer worth £9m to acquire Cambridge Instruments.[91] Rank argued that it could use its own selling network (which they admitted was under-utilised) to improve Cambridge's export performance. It had also noted that 'Cambridge has recently been re-organised to ensure its future profitability but this has not yet been reflected in the company's value'.[92] Rank's bid, however, was contested. On 16 May George Kent made a counter-bid of £11m.[93] The IRC took the view that the restructuring of the instruments industry would be better secured by a Kent take-over than a Rank purchase given Kent's 'right background of management and expertise'.[94]

Discussions with Kent's financial advisors (Lazards), however, convinced the IRC that Kent's 'did not have the financial strengths to win a battle with Rank.[95] At this point, the IRC took the decision to actively engage in market trading to ensure the success of the George Kent bid.[96] From then on market prices soared as the take-over battle ensued (Figure 4.3).

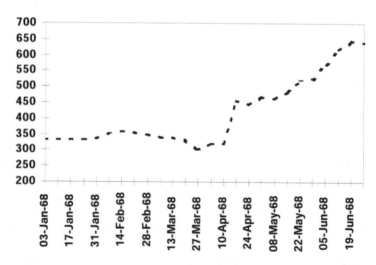

Figure 4.3 Cambridge Instrument Market Price (Old Pence)
Source: *Stock Exchange Gazette.*

The decision by the IRC to buy shares represents a further change in its strategy. Although the IRC did, in theory, have the authority under their Act to do this, this was the first time that the IRC had intervened *financially* in support of one party in a contested take-over bid.[97] It did so with the full knowledge of the DEA once that department had agreed to defend itself against the expected 'public storm' by an agreed public relations line . . . 'that the IRC has operational independence and what they are doing is based on their independent commercial judgement; the Secretary of State respects their judgement and sees no reason to intervene'.[98]

On 5 June the IRC released a press statement announcing their general support of Kent's improved offer.[99] What it did not announce was its decision to take an active part in share trading. By 11 June, as the take-over battle progressed, the IRC decided in private to acquire 'those Cambridge Instrument shares which are currently the property of the Trustees of the Royal Society . . . since this would give them a useful bargaining counter . . .'.[100] Two days later, the IRC had, in its own words 'crossed the Rubicon'. To ensure a victory for Kent's, the IRC had decided it was essential for them to have the 10 per cent holding of the Royal Society in addition to Kent's existing holding plus a 'few per cent more shares to be obtained on the market'. By midday of 13 June the IRC had obtained 2 per cent of the equity of the company 'but might get up to 5 per cent by the end of the day'. The estimated cost at this time was £2–£2.5m.[101] The same day, the IRC bought the Royal Society shareholding (11 per cent) at 55*s.* per share. In addition, it also bought additional Cambridge Instruments equity in the market. By Friday, 14 June, the IRC had acquired 100,750 ordinary shares of Cambridge Instruments at an average price of 54*s.* 10.06*d.*[102]

By this time, even officials at the DEA were beginning to feel that events were getting out of hand.[103] Their concerns were well founded. On the Monday (18 June), the IRC agreed to purchase 409,500 ordinary shares (8 per cent of equity of CSI) from Charterhouse, Japhet and Thomasson at 53*s.* 6*d.* a share, as well as 97,500 ordinary stock units of George Kent at an average price of 31*s.* 10*d.* each.[104] Not surprisingly, the same day Rank announced its withdrawal from the Cambridge bid as Lazards were able to announce that acceptances of the Kent offer had risen to over 55 per cent of the issued share capital of Cambridge.[105]

The IRC was able to ensure the success of its favoured candidate in the contested bid because it was able to acquire sufficient shares on the market to ensure the George Kent bid was accepted. Buying the shares of the Royal Society and of Charterhouse was obviously important. But its ability to buy shares on the open market was also crucial. It would be instructive to identify who sold those shares. It was private individuals rather than 'City' institutions that traded during the hectic month of June. During that month only three 'City' institutions sold their shares, two of which were nominee companies: London Royal Bank of Scotland Nominee (6,167 shares), The Scottish Union and National Insurance Company (50,000) and Standard Bank Nominees (6,457).[106] It was private individuals who gained from the escalating share price as the take-over battle raged.

This all meant that the IRC purchased, in total, 1,557,574 shares in Cambridge Instruments at a cost of £4,275,000 from the Royal Society, the Charterhouse Group and the market. They had also acquired in total 443,000 George Kent shares at a cost of £719,000 on the market in order to support their price and hence the value of Kent's final bid. The total gross cost was £5m.[107] In addition, the IRC had declared itself as a sub-underwriter for the Kent share offer, so that if 55 per cent of the shareholders elected to take the cash alternative, the IRC would be required to provide a further £1.3m.[108] This was to make the IRC the largest single shareholder in George Kent at September 1968. Its 2,921,662 ordinary shares gave the IRC 19.4 per cent of the company's ordinary shares.[109]

The third departure came with the contested bid for English Electric. When GEC announced its bid for AEI, there was no rival bidder. The battle for English Electric was a battle between Plessey and GEC. Plessey announced its bid on 21 August 1968.[110] For the first time in its history, the IRC took sides in the case of a *contested* bid. Although the IRC admitted that there was a case for it to 'be standing back and trying to determine a theoretical best structure for the industry against which the immediate situation could be reviewed', it decided against the stand back approach.[111] The IRC recommended that it (the IRC) should 'make every effort to bring about and should publicly support, a merger between EC and English Electric',[112] and thus made public its support for GEC's bid for English Electric.[113]

To do this, the IRC had to secure the agreement of a majority of English Electric shareholders. By April 1968, the top twenty shareholders in that company included the major insurance, pension and nominee companies who together held 23 per cent of the equity of English Electric (Table 4.9). The agreement of these major institutions was thus important to the success of the GEC bid. Three insurance companies were crucial to the AEI and the English Electric takeovers: the Prudential, the Co-Operative Insurance Company and Pearl Assurance. Their separate holdings in each of the three companies and their combined holdings after the mergers, indicate their general approval.

The take-over battle for English Electric was muted compared with that for AEI. Share prices rose (Figure 4.4), but the escalation that accompanied the AEI take-over was not witnessed in that of English Electric. The markets saw the wisdom of the GEC case (or more cynically decided not

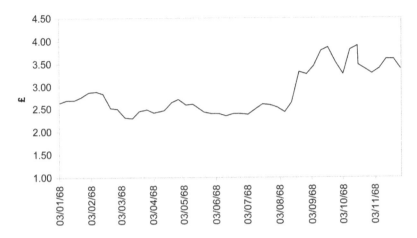

Figure 4.4 Share Prices: English Electric

Source: *Stock Exchange Gazette.*

to challenge an IRC supported bid). Supporting GEC and maintaining their equity holdings would best protect future dividend streams and asset values.

It is not without significance that the IRC took the decision to back GEC in private with the knowledge and agreement of the DEA, but without the knowledge or assent of other government departments. The IRC consulted the DEA and sent that department written notes of its views but the note was sent 'on a personal basis' with the typed preface that it was for a restricted audience and not be made public to other government departments. Government archives indicate that the DEA conformed to this request. Already, and dangerously, the IRC was beginning to operate a sole operation, which ran the risk of bringing it into conflict with other departments, and of inviting accusations of it being a law unto itself.

The switch of tactic to support in a contested bid was not the only new aspect to IRC strategy. It also wanted to make that support public, to 'hold equity in the new company, have a seat on the Board, and to extract promises of consultation by the Board with the Government and the IRC about the hiving off of fringe activities'.[114] The IRC was now beginning to extend its interests into the internal mechanisms of corporate governance through its desire to have representation on main company boards. This was a new and crucial departure. For those within government who wished to extend government influence, board representation on key industries was a positive development. But representation was not to be of or by Government but of and by the IRC. Again, the IRC ran the risk of being 'out of control'. The IRC was advised that whilst the transfer of loan stock into equity, Board presence and consultation were 'sensible', it was told in no uncertain terms that *public* support would not be welcomed by the Government.[115] Public support in a bid that was not contested (GEC and AEI) had provoked outcry – the Government did not wish to provoke the even greater outcry that would follow from public support in a contested bid.

In adopting a pro-active role in a contested take-over bid, the IRC ran the risk of opposition from industry in general to a restructuring which would determine the shape of the industry for many years to come, of provoking a counter-bid from Plessey in alliance with other companies in the industry, and of ministerial opposition from key Government departments. A counter-bid raised the spectre of the Government being involved in an open battle on the stock market: a prospect that civil servants and politicians did not relish. In the event, no such counter-bid occurred and the Government was saved the difficulties that an open battle would have raised.

The political climate favoured take-over bids and promised financial inducement to do so. Shareholders stood to gain: both from the terms offered and the promise of injection of funds into the newly merged companies. Future earnings would be best protected not by exiting but by increasing stakes in likely candidates. Standard take-over theories assume non-identical parties in the take-over process, with shareholders in the predator company being distinct from those of the acquired company. In practice, they are often the same. This applied in particular to those institutions, which had large shares in both, the acquired and the acquirer firm: notably the Prudential, the Co-Operative Insurance Society and Pearl Assurance (Table 4.10). By 1970, these and other financial institutions held large numbers of shares in the new GEC (Table 4.11).

The distribution of shareholding in each of the companies was such that no one shareholder held sufficient equity to dominate decision-making. Equally, many shareholders were persuaded of improved future earnings from the newly merged companies. All three bids prompted massive buying in the

Table 4.10 Holdings by the Prudential, The Co-Operative Insurance Society and Pearl Assurance in AEI, English Electric, GEC in 1967 and in GEC in 1969

Shareholder	GEC 1967	AEI 1967	English Electric 1967	GEC 1969
Prudential	2,750,014	2,245,018	2,048,725	17,358,994
Co-Operative	311,068	412,310	509,199	1,721,728
Pearl Assurance	452,212	268,956	500,160	2,569,324

Source: English Electric, General Electric Company and Associated Electrical Industries: Annual Returns of Shareholders at 1967 and (General Electric Company) 1969.

Table 4.11 Principal Institutional Shareholders in GEC, 1970

Prudential	19,710,270
Pearl Assurance	2,569,324
Union Pension Trust	1,396,960
Co-Op	1,721,728
Legal and General	1,660,388
Guardian Assurance	1,152,772
Norwich Union	1,150,153
Prudential Nominees	1,136,050
Equity & Law	1,000,000
Eagle Star	849,680

Source: General Electric Company: Annual Returns of Shareholders at 1970.

acquired companies as investors scrambled to gain from the anticipated gains from take-over. In the case of both AEI and English Electric, the anticipation focused on the financial benefits that would accrue from the imposition of the managerial skills of Weinstock, whose abilities had assumed almost mythical proportions in both Government and City circles. Public support from the IRC for GEC persuaded sufficient shareholders to ensure the success of its bid for English Electric and AEI. In the case of Cambridge Instruments, success for the IRC derived from its ability to buy shares from the Royal Society and Charterhouse, *but also* a considerable number of shares on the market.

The Wilson Government wanted to achieve rationalisation and modernisation of management in order to attain its ultimate objective of globally competitive industries. To do so, it had to persuade owners of industry to participate in and support take-overs. Given the unwillingness of the markets to respond to gentle persuasion, the Government took the decision to prompt structural change via take-overs, using the IRC as an intermediate agent that initiated and supported bids. They had not counted on the need for open buying on the markets to ensure success. Nor had they anticipated that such behaviour (and the overruling of majority patrician shareholders not supportive of take-over bids) would act in the interests of the 'new' institutional shareholders who, unlike the patrician institutions, interpreted ownership in rights rather than responsibilities and who pursued (with zeal and profit) their rights to trade shares and thereby optimise income from their assets.

VI

These modern initiatives and 'new' Labour thinking by 'old' Labour came to nought. The underlying reason was an inertia born of the complications of administrative solutions to internal mechanisms together with a general sense of alarm at the attempts of the IRC to determine the external mechanisms of corporate governance. The feeling that 'there was much to be said for leaving things as they were'[116] meant the issue of the meaning of shareholding was left in abeyance.[117] The policy of the implications of Government acquiring shares '. . . (not) as a result of a consistent policy but for a variety of different reasons' was allowed to continue.[118] By May 1967, the working party set up to consider the role of the firm in modern society and its relations with stakeholders was having 'serious' doubts as to whether it was necessary to set up such a commission so soon after the Jenkins Commission and, more to the point, whether there was time in the current life of that parliament to deal with the questions raised. The final stamp of disapproval came in the decision of the Prime Minister on 7th June that there should be no such enquiry.[119] By July of that year a ministerial meeting at the DEA had reached the conclusion that 'the broader question of company philosophy was a longer term exercise which needed very careful examination' and that 'it could be realistically argued that the pressures on parliamentary time would not make the longer term exercise possible in this Parliament'.[120]

The immediate reason was preoccupation with the economic crises of 1967. Devaluation marked the resurgence of the pre-eminence of the 'Treasury' view. That resurgence led to the quiet death of any proposals to question the nature of stakeholding or to re-think the role of the firm. From this time on, the Treasury view prevailed. And that view was that no such initiatives on stakeholding or shareholding should be pursued, and no Government agency should seek to spend public monies to ensure the success of any take-over, particularly when this ran the risk of precipitating take-over booms and alienating the 'City'. The initiatives crumbled not only in the face of the government's mounting economic difficulties and the resurgence of Treasury influence, but also from inter-departmental rivalry and from mounting worries about the behaviour of the IRC which alarmed politicians and civil servants at MinTech, DTI and the DEA. By September 1968, the President of the Board of Trade was noting his own concerns that the IRC 'might speed up its operations so as to go too far and too fast with its schemes of industrial reconstruction',[121] whilst the Treasury complained that the IRC had 'for a matter of months' been 'building up its activities substantially and casting its net wider' and requested that it should be asked to 'be more selective in its activities in the interests of keeping down public expenditure'.[122] The activities of the DEA and its brainchild, the IRC, were viewed as increasingly out of hand and liable to incur the risk of 'excessive' expenditure for a Government dealing with the economic and psychological costs of the 1967 devaluation. The DEA was abolished on 6 October 1969. A year later the IRC was wound up.

We can however also trace the failure to the inherent tensions between 'City' and Government that underpinned and ultimately constrained the ability of the Government to force through change in the exercise of ownership responsibility. Bargaining leverage essentially lay with the City rather than Government. Whilst Government could wield no credible threat of enhanced regulation of the financial institutions and whilst Government needed the confidence of the financial markets, gentle persuasion to reform the exercise of ownership responsibilities had little real meaning. Administrative solutions required a long term perspective, parliamentary time and an electorate happy to allocate time to the niceties of company law legislation: the Wilson Government had none of these at its disposal.

The failure of these initiatives left untouched the issue of the stakeholder firm. The examination of company philosophy in stakeholder terms was to vanish and not surface again until recent times. If there was a singular failure within Government, it was a reluctance to tackle the 'philosophical' issues inherent in reform of company law that might have influenced the internal mechanisms of corporate governance. Given current views on the importance of such mechanisms in securing optimal performance from management, this was a costly decision by the Government.[123] Its choice was an understandable, given time pressures, concern to concentrate on electorally popular issues and aversion to bureaucratic solutions. That choice, however, meant no new incentive systems (or legal constraints), which may have persuaded shareholders to adopt ownership responsibilities.

That choice (and its consequences) were compounded by the lessons learnt from the activities of the IRC. Instigation of take-over booms, explicit overruling of the views of 'patrician' institutions further encouraged arms length relations between owners and managers and a propensity by the former to exit if and when the company experienced problems. The perverse result of the IRC's activities was that it made it more rather than less likely for owners to engage in ownership responsibilities. The lesson from the IRC was that loyalty brought few financial rewards; on the contrary large sums of money were to be made from active trading. The City was not slow to realise and put into effect such lessons.

The concurrent results of the failure to reform internal mechanisms and the intervention in the markets created serious long-term implications. A vacuum of responsibility now applied to the ownership of the firm and a resultant emphasis on the rights rather than the responsibilities of ownership. Shareholders had learned that loyalty counted for little, that monies were to be made from active trading. Rights rather than responsibilities of ownership prevailed. This all added to the vacuum of responsibility that reached crisis proportions when the full scale of the crisis of Rolls-Royce became apparent in the autumn of 1970. Rolls-Royce's crisis emanated from

financial miscalculations as to the cost of the RB211 project. It also emanated, however, from an absence of ownership responsibilities by the major
shareholders (many of who exited before the final crisis). Abrogation of
ownership responsibility by shareholders meant that in the final analysis it
was Government and the major clearing banks who assumed responsibility.[124] From this, shareholders were to have their preference for exit rather
than voice reinforced: an under-performing company would ultimately
be rescued by Government (if deemed strategically important); there was
as such no incentive for shareholders to intervene. Whilst the structure of
shareholding was a major constraint on the exercise of ownership responsibilities, the policies of the Wilson Government reinforced and if anything
increased such constraints.

Take-over by government, engineered to promote modernisation through
rationalisation and the imposition of modern management, marked the end
of a patrician era of 'City' industry relations, dominated by the insurance
companies who held shares in major companies, but rarely thought to intervene or to maximise their asset values by share transactions. Take-over gave
full rein to a new breed of 'City' institutions, interested only in maximising
asset values. The opposition of the Prudential and Pearl Assurance to the
AEI/GEC merger counted for nothing in the face of sustained buying by
the new managers of nominee accounts: indeed the success of the latter
over the former acted to encourage the emphasis on trading in property
rights. The new breed of 'City' institutions exercised exit: not only when
given companies under-performed, but also if they believed other companies promised better returns and managers of industry were to have to live
with the 'short term' focus of the City and their emphasis on market prices
and dividend returns. By default, the Government had unleashed 'a latent
monster' neither it nor subsequent Governments could control.

The laudable aims of the Wilson government to rethink the role of the
firm in society and to embrace the notion of 'stake-holding' and to seek
modernisation and enhanced competitiveness through merger and take-over
crumbled in the face of mounting economic difficulties. The question of the
stakeholder firm and best practice in corporate governance was left dormant
for more than a decade. But more insidiously, the activities of its brainchild,
the IRC, were to backfire. Take-over, the IRC had demonstrated, could be
achieved through aggressive share trading and in the face of opposition
from the 'old' City institutions. The success of the IRC in forcing through
such take-overs gave vent to the new breed of 'City' managers whose interests lay in maximising short run returns, whose activities stressed exit rather
than voice, whose behaviour stressed the rights rather than the responsibilities of shareholding and who set a 'short term' agenda which has bedevilled
corporate governance in the UK ever since.

Notes

1 See, for example, S. N. Broadberry, *The Productivity Race: British Manufacturing in International Perspective, 1850–1990* (Cambridge: Cambridge University Press, 1997).
2 How this impacted on managerial deliberations and strategy is a matter of debate. In the 1960s, Marris noted how the threat of take-over did come to influence decision making at board level. See Robin Marris, *The Economic Theory of 'Managerial, Capitalism* (London: Macmillan, 1966). More recently, Chandler has claimed that financial rather than economic logic determined take-over activity with the result that newly formed companies failed to realise economies of scale or scope, with the inevitable adverse consequences for competitive performance. See Alfred D. Chandler, Jr, 'Managerial Enterprise and Competitive Capabilites', *Business History*, Vol. 34, No. 1 (January, 1992), pp. 11–41.
3 See for example, N. F. R. Crafts, 'Economic Growth' in N. F. R. Crafts and Nicholas Woodward (eds), *The British Economy Since 1945* (Oxford: Clarendon Press, 1991), pp. 261–290 and Charles Bean and, N. F. R. Crafts, 'British Economic Growth since 1945: Relative Economic Decline . . . and Renaissance' in Nicholas Crafts and Gianni Toniolo (eds), *Economic Growth in Europe Since 1945* (London: Centre for Economic Policy Research, 1996), pp. 131–172.
4 See, for a very strong exposition of this view, Will Hutton, *The State We're In* (London, 1995).
5 See Mark J. Roe, *Strong Owners, Weak Managers: The Political Roots of American Corporate Finance* (Princeton University Press: Princeton, New Jersey, 1994); Andrei Schleifer and Robert W. Vishny, 'Large shareholders and corporate control', *Journal of Political Economy*, Vol. 94, No. 3 (1986), pp. 461–488; Andrei Schleifer and Robert W. Vishny, 'Politicians and Firms', *Quarterly Journal of Economics*, Vol. 109 (1994), pp. 995–1025.
6 With the exception of Richard Roberts, 'Regulatory Responses to the Rise of the Market for Corporate Control in Britain in the 1950s', *Business History*, Vol. 34, No. 1, (January, 1992), pp. 183–200.
7 Roe, *Strong Owners, Weak Managers*; Schleifer and Vishny, 'Politicians' and 'Large Shareholders'.
8 Department of Economic Affairs, *The National Plan* (London: September, 1965), Cmnd. 2764, para 1, p. 1.
9 Ibid., para 2, p. 1.
10 Ibid., pp. 18–19.
11 Ibid., para 15, p. 47.
12 Proposed takeover of AEI by GEC, IRC: Industrial Studies and Investigations, 14 July 1967 to 21 January 1968: (London: Public Record Office), EW 27/293: Item 3, paras 5 and 6, p. 2.
13 *The National Plan*, para 21, pp. 48–9.
14 Ibid., para 39, p. 9 and para 38, p. 53.
15 Rationalisation of the Electrical Engineering Industry, Memorandum, 6 October 1967, EW27/293.
16 See Sue Bowden, 'Corporate Governance in a Political Climate: The Impact of Public Policy Regimes on Corporate Governance in the UK' in John Parkinson, Andrew Gamble and Gavin Kelly (eds), *The Political Economy of the Company* (Oxford: Portland, 2000).
17 The growth of the institutional investor resulted from the growing presence of pension houses and insurance companies. The growth of insurance and pensions

led to a massive inflow of funds into their accounts which led to a widening and deepening of their company share portfolios. Between 1963 and 1975 the proportion of shares held by persons fell from 54 per cent to 37.5 per cent. Committee to Review the Functioning of Financial Institutions, *Progress Report on the Financing of Industry and Trade* (London: 1977), para 69, p. 20; George Clayton and W. T. Osborn, *Insurance Company Investment: Principles and Policy* (London: George Allen and Unwin, 1965); W. A. Thomas, *The Finance of British Industry, 1918–1976*, (London, 1978); Committee to Review the Functioning of Financial Institutions, *Written Evidence by Insurance Company Associations* (London: April 1978), pp 1–48; Committee to Review, *Progress Report*, paras 69–71, pp. 20–21; Jonathan Charkham, *Keeping Good Company; A Study of Corporate Governance in Five Countries* (Oxford: Clarendon Press, 1994); Matthew Gaved, *Closing the Communications Gap: Disclosure and Institutional Shareholders* (London: Institute of Chartered Accountants, April, 1997); Matthew Gaved, *Ownership and Influence* (London: Institute of Management, London School of Economics, 1994); G. P. Stapleton, *Institutional Shareholders and Corporate Governance* (Oxford: Clarendon Press, 1996).

18 Committee to Review the Functioning of Financial Institutions, Written Evidence by the Stock Exchange, p. 9.
19 Committee to Review, *Progress Report*, 1977, pp. 69–70.
20 Campbell, 1990; John Parkinson, 'Company Law and Stakeholder Governance' in Kelly et al., *Stakeholder Capitalism*.
21 Charkham, *Good Company*, p. 106.
22 Committee to Review, para 2 (a), p. 180. Second Stage Evidence (Volume 4); *Written Evidence by the Bank of England.*
23 Committee to Review, *Progress Report*, para 70, p. 21.
24 Ibid., para 77, p. 23.
25 Ibid., para 75, p. 22.
26 See Albert O. Hirschman, *Exit, Voice and Loyalty; Responses to Decline in Firms, Organizations and States* (Cambridge, Mass., Harvard University Press, 1970).
27 For the residual rights hypothesis, see S. J. Grossman and O. D. Hart, 'An Analysis of the Principal Agent Problem', *Econometrica* (1983), Vol. 51, pp. 7–45; for the property right hypothesis see Colin Mayer 'Stock-Markets, Financial Institutions and Corporate Performance' in Dimsdale and Prevezer (eds) *Capital Markets.*
28 Quoted in Ben Pimlott, *Harold Wilson* (London: HarperCollins, 1993), p. 222. Was Wilson serious when he said this? Pimlott appears to believe so. Whether Wilson believed such views or not, the fact was that he had uttered such views – and that, as such, the City had reason to have reservations about him.
29 See Mark J. Roe, *Strong Owners, Weak Managers*, p. 201. Roe argues that these political considerations were crucial in explaining the aversion to voice options by financial institutions in the UK system up to the Thatcher era.
30 See for example, Crossman p. 45 (November 1964), p. 72 (February 1965). Wilson made a particularly strong commitment to avoid Devaluation at his first Guildhall speech as Prime Minister on 16 November 1964 see Pimlott, *Wilson*, p. 353.
31 Grossman and Hart, '[a 6, not a 9] Analysis'.
32 Mayer, for example, has argued that the main method by which outsiders exert control in the UK and the USA is through takeovers and has described the

take-over mechanism as an efficient system by which a large number of dispersed investors who would otherwise have little incentive to be involved in the
monitoring of corporations can exert control over corporate activities. See Mayer,
'Stock Markets', p. 188.
33 Committee to Review, Second Stage Evidence, Volume 1, *Written Evidence by
the Panel on Take-overs and Mergers*, 1979, para 8, p. 3.
34 Roberts, *Regulatory Responses*.
35 Committee to Review, Second Stage Evidence, Volume 1, *Written Evidence by
the Panel on Take-overs and Mergers*, 1979, para 11, p. 4.
36 Through the early 1960s the Jenkins Commission had considered company law
and its main proposals were embedded in the Companies Act of 1967. There
were, however, 'fundamental questions relating to the operation of companies'
which the Commission did not consider because 'it was not concerned with
these wider issues of public policy', Inquiry into the Functions of the Company
in Modern Society: EW27/242, 11 November 1966.
37 The functions of the company in modern society: EW 27/242, 7.12.1966.
38 Ibid., p. 10: EW27/242.
39 Ibid., p. 3: EW27/242.
40 Committee on the Financial Aspects of Corporate Governance, *Draft Report*
(1992). (Cadbury Committee)
41 File note of 5 April 1965 on company law reform: Company Law Reform:
EW27/4
42 Ibid.
43 Note of 2 December 1966: (London: PRO), Investment Grants Steering Group:
Papers and Briefs: EW26/42
44 Submission from the Registrar of Companies, 29 March 1960 (London: PRO),
Company Law Committee: Oral Evidence, 28 October 1960: BT147/22
45 Note by the Treasury, prepared 2 December 1966: (London, PRO) Ad Hoc
Group on Departmental Responsibility for Government Shareholdings:
EW26/77.
46 Note by the Treasury, prepared 2 December 1966: EW26/77.
47 Minutes of Meeting, 18 January 1967: EW26/77.
48 Ibid.
49 Government Shareholding in Mixed Enterprises: Interim Report by the DEA, 4
May 1967: The Government's Purpose in Acquiring Shares in a Company and
The Government's Rights as a Shareholder: EW 26/77.
50 The Labour Government established the IRC as an independent statutory body in
1966. Its remit was to 'increase industrial efficiency and profitability and assist
the UK economy by promoting industrial reorganisation and development'. IRC
Financial Policy. Draft, 5 June 1968 (London: PRO), IRC, Financial Policy, Papers
from 1.6.1968 to 31.10.1968: EW2/10. It had a remit to 'promote or assist the reorganisation or development of any industry and, at the request of the Secretary of
State, to establish or develop, or promote or assist the establishment or development of any industrial enterprise'. IRC Corporation Act 1967, Appendix A, EW
26/42; IRC Financial Policy, Draft 5 June 1968, EW 2/10. Aris sees the IRC as a
government-sponsored merchant bank, the idea of which was borrowed from the
Italian Instituto per la Riconstruzione Industriale. See Stephen Aris, *Arnold Weinstock and the Making of GEC* (London: Aurum Press, 1998), p. 60.
51 Draft brief for Secretary of State's meeting with IRC, 27 October 1967, IRC
Policy: EW27/291.

52 Ibid.
53 Ibid.
54 GEC/AEI: Rationalisation of the Electrical Engineering Industry. 12 October 1967. (London: PRO), Merger between AEI and GEC, EW27/293. The record of the IRC's achievements in this respect has largely been written in terms of its own personnel and on the basis of a case study approach of each of the main industries it was involved in. See Douglas Hague and Geoffrey Wilkinson, 'GEC, AEI and English Electric' in Hague and Wilkinson, *The IRC – An Experiment in Industrial Intervention* (Hemel Hempstead, Herts: Allen and Unwin, 1983), Part 2, Chapter 4, pp. 49–71. Yet the files of the IRC, together with those of the Board of Trade (DTI), the Ministry of Technology (MinTech) and the Treasury can be used more fruitfully to identify the problems of rectifying corporate governance at this time.
55 Draft brief for Secretary of State's meeting with IRC, 27 October 1967, EW 27/291.
56 IRC, Statement, 9 September 1968 (London: PRO), GEC/English Electric: Correspondence from 1 August to 19 September 1968, EW26/69, p. 1.
57 Rationalisation of the Electrical Engineering Industry, 12 October 1967, EW 27/293. The National Plan noted that 'the proportion of output going to exports has been gradually declining over the years to approximately 16 per cent currently, at the same time as the industry has obtained a declining proportion of world trade in electrical engineering products'. *The National Plan*, para 20, pp. II–103. Imports meanwhile had grown and 'the possible serious implications of the rapid rise in the rate of imports are now evident'. *The National Plan*, para 22, pp. II–103.
58 *The National Plan*, para 26, pp. II–104.
59 IRC, Statement, 9 September 1968, EW 26/69, p. 1.
60 See Aris, *Weinstock*, pp. 61–3 for a retrospective assessment of the performance of AEI which concurs with the contemporary analysis of government officials.
61 Note by IRC for DEA on Plessey Bid for English Electric, EW 26/69, 3 September 1968, p. 11.
62 Mergers Panel: Proposed Acquisition, Notes, 10 May 1968, George Kent and Cambridge Instruments Merger, Papers from 10 May 1968 to 19 June 1968: EW26/60, para. 4.
63 Robert Jones and Oliver Marriott, *Anatomy of a merger: a history of GEC, AEI and English Electric* (London: Cape, 1970); Hague and Wilkinson, *The IRC*; Alex Brummer and Roger Cowe, *Weinstock: The Life and Times of Britain's Premier Industrialist* (London: HarperCollins, 1998).
64 *Investors Chronicle*, 6 January 1967, p. 9
65 *Investors Chronicle*, 3 March 1967, p. 665.
66 *Stock Exchange Gazette*, 13 January 1967, 104; *Investors Chronicle*, 3 March 1967, p. 694.
67 If there was a takeover bid, then the chances were that the 'aggressor' company would seek to buy shares at a higher price. A merged company (say of AEI and GEC) could also lead to enhanced share values.
68 The initial bid by GEC for AEI was £120m. At the then existing market prices, this placed a value of about 53s. on the AEI shares; they were worth 43s. 6d. immediately before the proposed bid was announced. Background Facts and Estimates for Mergers Panel, EW 27/293.
    The bid was subsequently raised to £152m on 29 October and £162m on 1 November 1967. Brief for Secretary of State's lunch with AEI, EW 27/293.

Plessey's bid for EE was valued at £260m Plessey/English Electric, undated. EW26/69. Rank's £9m bid for Cambridge represented a value of 35*s*. 9*d*. per share. Mergers Panel: Proposed Acquisition, Notes, 10 May 1968, EW 26/60; *Investors Chronicle* and *Stock Exchange Gazette*, 17 May 1968, p. 684. Rank subsequently raised its offer to 47*s*. 10.5*d*. per share. *Investors Chronicle* and *Stock Exchange Gazette*, 31 May 1968, p. 915.

69 Letter from Weinstock to Harold Wilson, 6 November 1967, PREM13/2797.

70 Ibid.

71 Aris, *Weinstock*, p. 63–4.

72 Ibid., p. 64.

73 Letter from Weinstock to Harold Wilson, 6 November 1967, PREM13/2797.

74 See, Aris, *Weinstock*, p. 65.

75 The timing was linked to the publication of AEI's half yearly figures which documented the company's profit fall back (from £6.9 million to £3.7 million). See Aris, *Weinstock*, pp 65–6.

76 Mergers Panel, Proposed Acquisition by GEC of AEI: Paper containing background facts and estimates. EW27/293.

77 Note of 6 November 1968, PREM 13/2797.

78 The merged company 'would create a group with strong representation across virtually the whole range of electrical and electronic products which would have the financial, marketing and research resources to match those of our main overseas competitors'. Note for the President of the Board of Trade, 16 October 1967, EW 27/293.

79 'GEC has the "new broom" type of management and it could undoubtedly make better use of the AEI assets than can the present management of that company'. Merger between AEI/GEC File Notes, 3 October 1967, EW 27/293. GEC management had 'demonstrated their ability to eliminate unprofitable activities and select and develop operations of maximum profitability . . . '[a 9, not a 6]. With this management added to that of AEI, the . . . 'resources of the combined group would be re-deployed in a way which was likely to increase greatly the group's efficiency and profitability and hence raise the competitive pressure on the rest of the industry.' Note for the President of the Board of Trade, 16 October 1967, EW 27/293.

80 The share registers cover a 15-month period up to 26 September 1968. AEI, Annual Return made up to 26 September 1968.

81 Amongst the institutions, the 44,500 shares sold by Legal and General explain the dominanceof the insurance companies.

82 See Brummer and Cowe, *Weinstock*, p 115. See their account of the battle on pp. 107–120. Aris concurs that 'though the issue was ultimately decided in the marketplace, the IRC's public support was crucial'. Aris, *Weinstock*, p. 67.

83 The then head of the IRC

84 Private Office Minute, No. 934, 2 November 1967, FV11/2.

85 Brummer and Cowe, *Weinstock*, p. 117.

86 Comment by the Secretary of State (DEA) at a meeting between the Secretary of State and his officials (DEA) together with representatives of the IRC, 31 May 1968: EW26/60.

87 The Government was well aware of the fact that the leading institutional shareholders were 'very much divided in their views', with 'no indication that (they) acted together on the takeover bid'. Note by the Board of Trade for the Adjournment Debate: EW27/293.

88 Brummer and Cowe, *Weinstock*, p. 118.

89 Ibid.
90 Proposed Acquisition of Cambridge Instrument Co. Ltd by the Rank Organisation, Mergers Panel G2 954/63, 10 May 1968: EW 26/60, p. 9.
91 Proposed Acquisition of Cambridge Instrument Co. Ltd by the Rank Organisation, Mergers Panel G2 954/63, 10 May 1968: EW 26/60, p. 9.
92 Ibid., p. 10.
93 Mergers Panel: Proposed Acquisition of Cambridge Instruments Co. Ltd by George Kent Ltd 22nd May 1968, paras. 1 and 2, EW 26/60.
94 File note of 30 May 1968: EW26/60.
95 Ibid.
96 Notes for the Secretary of State, 5 July 1968: George Kent and Cambridge Instruments Merger, Papers from Assistance to Fairfields: Nominal A-Z Aid, 20 June 1968, EW26/61.
97 Minutes of a meeting between MinTech and the DEA, 14 June 1968: EW27/291. This was the line adopted by the DEA at its meeting with the Treasury and MinTech on 14 June 1968 (EW 26/60: Notes of meeting on 14 June 1968). The Secretary of State for Economic Affairs admitted to the Prime Minister that 'this is the first occasion on which the IRC has given financial support to influence the outcome of a contested take-over and inevitably controversy has arisen'. He was to defend the actions of the IRC on the grounds that 'the Corporation would lose much of its authority if it were known that it would retire from the contest immediately a third party entered the arena'. Note by Secretary of State for Economic Affairs for the Prime Minister, 19 June, 1968, PREM 13/2247.
98 DEA File note of 31 May 1968: EW 26/60.
99 DEA File note of 5 June 1968: EW26/60.
100 DEA File note of 11 June 1968: notes of a telephone conversation between the DEA and the IRC: EW26/60.
101 Note of a telephone conversation, DEA and IRC, 13 June 1968: EW 26/60.
102 IRC Press Announcement, 17 June 1968: EW26/60.
103 DEA, File note of 18 June 1968. This noted that events were 'moving so fast that even oral reports and certainly not paper reports can barely keep up with it'. EW26/60.
104 Press Announcement by IRC, Noon, 18 June 1968: EW 26/60.
105 Lazards, Press Announcement, 10.30 a.m. 18 June 1968: EW 26/60.
106 George Kent Limited, *Annual Report and Register of Shareholders*, 1967–1969 inclusive (Companies House, London), Ref: 06223.
107 Note by Secretary of State for Economic Affairs for the Prime Minister, 19 June 1968, PREM13/2247.
108 Treasury note estimating the cost of the IRC intervention, 24 June 1968: EW26/60.
109 George Kent Limited, *Annual Register of Shareholders* as at 18 September 1968. Its nearest 'rivals' were Pension Fund Securities (260,311), Sun Life (217,916) and Royal Insurance (213,208). Although these activities 'sailed close to the mark' they did not infringe the City's new Code on Take-overs and Mergers published on 27 March 1968: EW26/61.
110 The IRC became involved for three reasons. First, because the bid 'raised some fundamental questions about the desirable structure for the whole electrical/electronics industry' which, given the 'duties entrusted to it by Parliament', meant the IRC could not 'avoid the responsibility of forming a view'. Second, the IRC had made a £15m loan to English Electric at the time of its merger with

Elliott Automation. The terms of this loan allowed the IRC to demand repayment (at a premium of 15 per cent) in the event of English Electric becoming a subsidiary of another company. Finally, the IRC became involved, because Plessey asked for its support and English Electric asked for advice. IRC, Statement, 9 September 1968, p. 2, EW26/69. Although the IRC had known that GEC had wanted to take over English Electric from June 1968. Note for the Record 5 September 1968, PREM 13/2797. Government archives thus show that IRC knew about Weinstock's plans in relation to EE one month earlier than the dating given by Aris. See Aris, *Weinstock*, p. 78.

111 The Electrical Electronics Industry: The Plessey Bid for English Electric, Note sent by the IRC to the DEA 'on a personal basis' 3 September 1968, EW 26/69, para 8, p. 3. Plessey, moreover, was smaller (though more profitable) than its target and, as Aris discussed, the logic of a Plessey/EE merger was not compelling given the absence of real industrial match between the two companies. See Aris, *Weinstock*, p. 78.

112 The Electrical Electronics Industry: The Plessey Bid for English Electric, Note sent by the IRC to the DEA 'on a personal basis' with the instruction that it 'not be shown or mentioned to other departments'. 3 September 1968, EW 26/69.

113 IRC: Statement for Publication, EW 26/69. The decision of the IRC to back GEC was based on 'what is financially practicable, what is industrially sensible from a national interest standpoint and what is practicable, having regard to the abilities and views of the managements of the major companies involved or likely to be involved.' The Electrical Electronics Industry: The Plessey Bid for English Electric, Note sent by the IRC to the DEA 'on a personal basis' 3 September 1968, EW 26/69, para 9, p. 3. Plessey was seen as being less strong financially than GEC that alone had the financial strength and industrial importance to take over English Electric. The Electrical Electronics Industry: The Plessey Bid for English Electric, 3 September 1968, EW 26/69, paras 10 and 11, pp. 3–4. Industrial logic supported a GEC rather than a Plessey take-over of English Electric. It was important to create the strongest possible company to compete in the international market in the electronics market, whilst there was urgent need for rationalisation of the heavy electrical side. GEC rather than Plessey could best achieve these aims. The Electrical Electronics Industry: The Plessey Bid for English Electric, Note sent by the IRC to the DEA 'on a personal basis' 3 September 1968, EW 26/69, para 23, p. 10. Finally, the IRC had implicit faith in the superior management skills of GEC in general and of its chief executive, Weinstock, in particular. The Plessey management was described as 'not generally recognised as being in the Weinstock class.' Finally, the IRC had implicit faith in the superior management skills of GEC in general and of its chief executive, Weinstock, in particular. The Plessey management was described as 'not generally recognised as being in the Weinstock class.'

114 Notes of a meeting 6 Sept 1968 between the Minister of Technology and the IRC. EW 26/69.

115 Ibid.

116 Minutes of Meeting, 5 January 1967: EW26/77.

117 Minutes of Meeting 18 January 1967, EW 26/77.

118 Minutes of Meeting 5 January 1967, EW26/77.

119 File note, 7th June 1967: EW 27/242.

120 Notes of a Meeting at the DES, Minister of State Office Minute No. 402, 5 July 1967: EW27/242.

121 Extract from Sept (68) Meeting, p. 6 and File note, 17 September 1968, para 5, pp 7–8: EW26/69

122 Letter from the Treasury to the DEA, 21 June 1968: EW2/10.

123 See Martin Conyon and Dennis Leech, 'Top pay, company performance and corporate governance', *Oxford Bulletin of Economics and Statistics*, 56 (1994), pp. 229–245; M. Conyon, P. Gregg and S. Machin, 'Taking care of business: executive compensation in the United Kingdom', *Economic Journal*, 105 (1995), pp. 704–714.

124 See Department of Trade and Industry, 1972 and 1973.

Index

Page numbers in **bold** refer to figures, page numbers in *italic* refer to tables

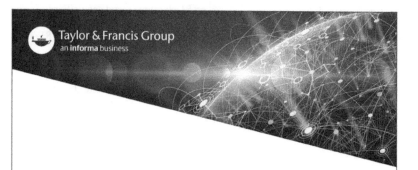